RICHARD NIXON
A POLITICAL LIFE

RICHARD NIXON
A POLITICAL LIFE

RICHARD M. PIOUS

JULIAN MESSNER

Copyright © 1991 by Richard M. Pious

All rights reserved including the right of reproduction in whole or in part in any form.
Published by Julian Messner, a division of Silver Burdett Press, Inc., Simon & Schuster, Inc., Prentice Hall Bldg., Englewood Cliffs, NJ 07632.

Julian Messner and colophon are trademarks of Simon & Schuster, Inc.
Designed by Michael J. Freeland.

Manufactured in the United States of America.

Lib. ed. 10 9 8 7 6 5 4 3 2 1
paper ed. 10 9 8 7 6 5 4 3 2 1

Library of Congress Cataloging-in-Publication Data
Pious, Richard M.
Richard M. Nixon / Richard M. Pious.
p. cm.
Includes bibliographical references and index.
Summary: Traces the life and career of the American president who was forced to resign after the Watergate scandal.
1. Nixon, Richard M. (Richard Milhous), 1913- —Juvenile literature. 2. Presidents—United States—Biography—Juvenile literature. 3. United States—Politics and government—1945- —Juvenile literature. [1. Nixon, Richard M. (Richard Milhous), 1913- . 2. Presidents.] I. Title.
E856.P56 1991
973.924'092—dc20
[B] 91-13013
CIP
AC
ISBN 0-671-72852-0 (LSB) ISBN 0-671-72853-9 (paper)

CONTENTS

	PREFACE: "BRING US TOGETHER"	vii
1.	CALIFORNIA DREAMIN'	1
2.	CLIMBING CAPITOL HILL	11
3.	ON THE NATIONAL TICKET	21
4.	A HEARTBEAT AWAY	29
5.	HARD LOSSES	37
6.	THE ROAD TO THE WHITE HOUSE	49
7.	WAR AND PEACE	61
8.	DOMESTIC POLICY	71
9.	CRIMES AND MISDEMEANORS	81
10.	THE NIXON PRESIDENCY	95
	IMPORTANT DATES IN THE LIFE OF RICHARD M. NIXON	101
	FURTHER READING	105
	INDEX	109

PREFACE
"BRING US TOGETHER"

At noon on January 20, 1969, Richard Milhous Nixon stood at a podium at the U.S. Capitol. His left hand rested on an open Bible and his right was raised as he met the gaze of Earl Warren, Chief Justice of the United States. It was Warren's duty to administer the oath that would formally mark the beginning of Nixon's first term as thirty-seventh president of the United States. Nixon, echoing the words that Warren spoke, pledged to "preserve, protect and defend the Constitution of the United States."

Nixon then faced a much larger audience. It included hundreds of public figures who had been invited to Washington, D.C., this bleak winter day to observe the new president's inauguration and were now seated before him. Among the audience were also millions of ordinary citizens at home before their television sets, the same sets on which they heard each night the latest news about the Vietnam War.

Thousands of American troops had died in that conflict and, with no end in sight, the nation was bitterly divided. Some called for a greater show of military force that would bring a quick end to the war, others for immediate withdrawal. Nixon himself promised to end the war. "The greatest honor history can bestow is the title of peacemaker," he told his vast audience. He pledged to lead the nation to "that high ground of peace."

There was violence at home as well. Antiwar demonstrations had pitted protesters against police. More alarming yet were the full-scale riots in many cities in which blacks and whites had met in angry confrontation. Nixon called on Americans to move forward in unison, "black and white together, as one nation, not two."

To Democrats and Republicans, liberals and conservatives, prowar hawks and antiwar doves, Nixon argued that "we cannot learn from one another until we stop shouting at one another." Nixon saw his mission as being to answer a plea he had heard during the campaign, when a supporter had held up a sign that asked the Republican candidate, now the president, "to bring us together." Nixon then concluded his first presidential address on a note of hope.

Five years and seven months later—on August 8, 1974—President Nixon gave his last such address, this time to announce his resignation from office. He remains the only president ever to have done so. He had no choice. If he had not resigned he would have been removed by impeachment, for he had betrayed the oath of office he had sworn to uphold and had fallen into scandal, corruption, and crime. It was a fall without parallel, perhaps the most dramatic in American history. It could have happened only to a remarkable man.

1

California Dreamin'

Richard Milhous Nixon came from an ordinary American family. He grew up in a family without wealth, fame, or influence. The members of his family were hard working, religious, and self-reliant—typical of their time and place.

THE FAMILY TREE
Richard Nixon's ancestors on his mother's side, the Milhouses, were Germans who moved to England in the seventeenth century and later to Ireland. There they converted to a new religion, the Religious Society of Friends, better known as the Quakers. The members of this faith did not congregate in churches or obey the teachings of priests. They worshipped instead at what were called meetings—sessions of silent meditation and prayer, in which every person was treated as an equal. Today, Quakers still worship in this same manner. They are usually pacifists, most of whom refuse to bear arms in wartime.

The Milhouses immigrated to America in 1729. They settled in Pennsylvania and remained there for more than a hundred years, then moved to Indiana and later Ohio. It was in Ohio that Hannah Milhous, Richard Nixon's mother, was born, in 1885. In 1897 her parents—Richard's grandparents—make a bold move. They joined the waves of working and middle-class families who were then leaving the "snowbelt" states of the Midwest and headed for the warmth and greenery of California. The Milhouses made their new home in Whittier, a small suburb southeast of Los Angeles.

Richard's family on his father's side, the Nixons, were English Methodists who came to America in 1731. They settled first in Delaware, where they farmed. The Nixons were neither Quakers nor pacifists. Nixons fought in the War of Independence and later in the Civil War, for the North. A Nixon fell in the battle of Gettysburg.

Frank Nixon, Richard's father, was born in 1878. He grew up on a forty-acre farm in Ohio. His family was penniless, so at age seven Frank was packed off to live with an uncle in Columbus. He did not enter a classroom until he was nearly fourteen, and then lasted only a few months. As a young man he worked for a time in Colorado as a rancher before returning to Columbus, where he then worked as a motorman on a streetcar. However, he was fired during a dispute over working conditions. In 1907 he migrated to Los Angeles. Again he took a job as a motorman and again he was fired, this time because the vehicle he was driving struck a car. He next found a new job as a ranch foreman.

Meanwhile, Frank Nixon had met Hannah Milhous at a Quaker Valentine's party. They were not social equals. Hannah's family was middle class. Frank, who had no family in the area, belonged to the working class. He was boisterous and loud, traits frowned upon by the Quakers, though he had recently been accepted into their faith. Hannah's family had misgivings about him. The couple were determined, however, and were married in 1908, four months after they met. They had four children, all boys. Richard Milhous, their second son, was born on January 9, 1913.

THE EARLY YEARS

Richard's parents lived at first in a small bungalow in Yorba Linda, a Quaker agricultural community. Frank raised lemons on land his father-in-law gave him. He also taught in a Quaker Sunday school, where he emphasized the values of hard work, Christian morality, and good citizenship. The Nixons were poor, but Frank was always a hard worker and earned extra money as a carpenter and handyman. He helped build the town's citrus warehouse and many of its homes. His sons pitched in, too. Richard and his brother Donald worked as fruit pickers in their father's lemon groves, and helped by hoeing weeds and irrigating the groves. But their labors came to nothing, for the lemon grove failed.

School was another matter. Richard succeeded there from the time he entered the first grade, in 1919. He was a good reader and had an outstanding memory. His teachers were so impressed with him that they promoted him directly from the first grade to the third. He continued to bring home perfect report cards.

At night Richard listened to the sounds of the trains leaving Yorba Linda for the large cities beyond. He dreamed of becoming a railroad engineer and seeing the world outside his small town. It was, for the time being, a distant dream. Times were hard for the Nixons.

In 1923 the family moved to the nearby town of East Whittier and opened Frank Nixon's General Merchandise store. Customers stopped by to purchase food and discuss politics with Frank, a loyal Republican. Richard, who put in many hours at the store, shared his father's passion for

Frank and Hannah Nixon and their children—from left, Harold, Donald, and Richard—in Yorba Linda, California, 1916.

politics. When he was eleven a scandal erupted in Washington that implicated members of the cabinet in bribery and corruption. "When I grow up," Richard promised his mother, "I'm going to be a lawyer they can't bribe so things like that can't happen."

Richard's boyhood was a mixture of tragedy and triumph. His most painful setback was the death of his brother Arthur, in August 1925, at the age of seven, just when Richard was entering the eighth grade. "For weeks after Arthur's funeral there was not a day that I did not think about him and cry," he recalled in his memoir. Richard pressed on, though. He became president of his class, played on the soccer team, was voted its most outstanding member, and graduated first in his class.

Richard did just as well at Whittier Union High School as he had in grade school. His marks there were excellent, even though he arose every morning at four-thirty to drive the family truck into Los Angeles, where he picked up produce for his father's store. At school, Richard went out for football (he sat on the bench), played the violin in the orchestra, and starred on the debate team. In his junior year he ran for student body president but lost to a varsity football player who was better looking and more popular. The loser graduated, however, with an award that named him the best all-around student.

Sorrow then struck the Nixon family again. Richard's brother Harold came down with tuberculosis. Hannah Nixon left the rest of her family behind and took Harold four hundred miles away, to Prescott, Arizona, where she hoped he would recover in the dry desert air. Richard joined them in the summers and got a job there as a barker at a nearby

Nixon's high school graduation photo, taken in 1930.

carnival. His concession was called Dick's Wheel of Fortune. It made more money than any other booth.

COLLEGE AND LAW SCHOOL

Gradually, Frank Nixon's business picked up. He was able to buy a gas station. The profits from it and the grocery store made it possible for him to afford two cars, a luxury in 1930, when the Great Depression had begun. He also was able to send Richard to Whittier College, a small Quaker school with four hundred students. It offered a wide array of activities, many of which Richard participated in. He was on the football team, excelled on the debating squad, and joined the drama society to act in several plays. He continued to get top grades, majoring in history, even though he still logged hours behind the counter of his father's grocery store and made his usual early-morning drives to Los Angeles in the produce truck.

Richard's favorite activity at Whittier College was politics. In his freshman year he was elected to the student council on a platform that called for more student rights and privileges. He also organized a fraternity, then sponsored the admission of a black student. It was the first time an African American had ever been invited to join a fraternity anywhere in California. In his junior year Richard won election as student body vice-president. Yet he was quite shy, with no close friends. In the spring of his junior year, his brother Harold died. "From that time on," Hannah Nixon later told a writer for *Good Housekeeping* magazine, "it seemed that Richard was trying to be three sons in one." In his grief he plunged into politics. He was elected president of the student body and talked of his ambition "to become a congressman."

Nixon graduated from Whittier College in 1934. He

ranked second in his class and won a scholarship to Duke Law School, in North Carolina, across the country. To save money there Nixon lived in cheap boardinghouses and at one point even moved into an abandoned toolshed that had no heat or running water. As always, he held part-time jobs, in this case chauffeuring the invalid wife of a law professor and working in the law library. Again as always, he studied hard. For his first year he recorded an A average, and his scholarship was renewed in full. He continued to pursue his interest in politics. In 1936–37, his third and final year of law school, Nixon became president of the student bar association (a form of student government) by promising that the association would help students find employment after graduation. Ironically, he could have used its help himself.

During the Christmas holiday of 1936, Nixon visited New York City and applied for jobs there with large firms. He had good credentials: he ranked third in his law class. Duke was only a small, new school in the South, however, and the old-line firms in Manhattan were like exclusive clubs. They preferred graduates from the prestigious law schools of the Northeast, such as Harvard, Yale, and Columbia. Besides, these were still hard times—the Depression had not yet ended—and jobs remained scarce. The two top-ranking students at Duke landed jobs in New York, but Nixon did not. He next applied for a job with the Federal Bureau of Investigation (FBI) but again was turned down.

Nixon's only remaining option was to return to California to practice law. There he passed the state bar exam, in November 1937 at the age of twenty-four, and shortly thereafter started work with the small Whittier firm of Wingert and Bewley.

FROM WHITTIER TO WASHINGTON

Whittier was not New York. Its population was only 25,000 people, and the legal work that came Nixon's way was small cases. He was a good trial lawyer, though, and became a partner in the firm in 1939. But he remained an unknown lawyer—and an underpaid one. In fact, he still lived with his parents and worked part-time in their store. At this point he tried a get-rich-quick scheme, investing all his savings in a company he organized to market frozen orange juice. The company failed, however, and left him broke.

Nixon was not, however, at a dead end. He continued to pursue his public activities. He was chosen president of both California's Duke alumni association and the Whittier College Alumni Association. He also was on the board of trustees of Whittier College.

Politically, Nixon kept as busy as ever. He was elected president of the Whittier Young Republicans and addressed civic groups. His ongoing theme was the failures of the Democratic administration of President Franklin D. Roosevelt. Nixon hoped to win Republican party nomination for the state legislature. That did not happen—but something better did.

In 1938, in a local theater group at Whittier, Richard Nixon met Thelma Catherine—known as "Pat"—Ryan. Pat Ryan came from a poor farm family in Artesia, nine miles south of Whittier. She had earned a degree in business from Fullerton Junior College, worked as a bank teller, and then gone to New York City, where she had found a job at a hospital as an X-ray technician. When that ended, she returned to California and enrolled at the University of Southern California in Los Angeles. There she studied merchandising and graduated with honors in 1937. She also earned extra money in Hollywood as a movie extra. When Nixon met her, Pat was teaching evening classes in shorthand and other business subjects at his old school, Whittier Union High. On weekends she commuted to Los Angeles, where she had an active social life.

"For me," Nixon later recalled, "it was a case of love at first sight." In *Richard Milhous Nixon: The Rise of an American Politician,* Roger Morris wrote that after their third meeting at the theater group Nixon blurted out to Pat, "Someday I'm going to marry you." This proved to be easier said than done. Pat, a high-spirited young woman, refused to go out with the earnest young lawyer. Richard Nixon remained persistent. If Pat was not interested in a date, very well, he would call on her anyway and take her for a drive or a long walk. Did she want to spend the weekend in Los Angeles and see other men? Fine: Nixon drove her there on Fridays and brought her back to Whittier on Sundays. In short, he refused to give up. As Pat got to know Nixon she came to admire him. Finally, on June 27, 1940, they were married in the presidential suite of a local hotel.

The bride and groom both wanted more out of life than Whittier could offer, however. In the fall of 1941 Nixon accepted a job in Washington, D.C., as a lawyer with the Office of Price Administration (OPA), a federal agency that regulated consumer prices. Nixon's job would be minor, but at least it put him in the nation's capital, near the hub of government. It happened that on Sunday, December 7, after a day spent packing for the move to Washington, the couple relaxed at a movie. As they left the theater, a boy was hawking a late edition of the local newspaper. "Japanese Bomb Pearl Harbor!" the headlines read. "We're at war, mister," the newsboy exclaimed.

2

CLIMBING CAPITOL HILL

Richard Nixon's first assignment in Washington with the Office of Price Administration (OPA) was to review the regulations that rationed government tires to motorists and truckers. He handled this task efficiently and moved on to more challenging ones. By the summer of 1942 he was promoted and given a raise.

SERVICE IN THE PACIFIC
Nixon was entitled to sit out the war because, as a Quaker, he was a pacifist. However, he did not want to do so. His commitment to the war effort ultimately outweighed his religious beliefs. In August 1942 he enrolled in the Navy's officer candidate school and was commissioned a lieutenant, junior grade (jg). He was posted first to Iowa, where he helped run a naval air station. Pat stayed behind in Washington to work for the OPA. Her business training had come in handy there. After seven months in Iowa, Nixon was reassigned to the South Pacific. He did not see combat but worked at supply and transport airfields. His base, at Bougainville, in the Solomon Islands, suffered a heavy attack

from the Japanese in December 1943. After it, Nixon helped clear corpses from a wrecked bomber.

Nixon proved to be a popular officer. Among other things, he opened "Nick's snack shack," which served hamburgers to his men. He scrounged up extra supplies for them and even offered classes in business law for those who were thinking of new careers. He also became a shrewd poker player who not only won but saved several thousand dollars. In July 1944, when Nixon returned to the United States, he had two battle stars and a glowing evaluation from his commanding officer. He was promoted to lieutenant commander in 1945, then spent several months in Philadelphia and New York doing legal work.

THE FIRST CAMPAIGN

"I am writing you this short note to ask if you would like to be a candidate for Congress on the Republican ticket in 1946." This note reached Nixon on September 30, 1945. It came from Herman Perry, manager of the Whittier branch of the Bank of America and a leading local Republican. Nixon discussed the matter with Pat and sent an enthusiastic telegram to Perry. On November 2, Nixon flew to California to meet the members of the Committee of 100, a group of wealthy contributors to the Republican party from California's twelfth congressional district. They were impressed by the young Navy veteran and on November 28 nominated him for election to Congress. At last he would become a professional politician.

Nixon's first test was a tough one. He was young, inexperienced, and a Republican in a district that had a slight majority of Democrats. Worse, the incumbent, Democrat Jerry Voorhis, was popular. Nixon was the underdog, but he did not mind. As was his custom, he worked extremely hard. He campaigned every day, including February 21, the day his first child, Tricia, was born. (A second daughter, Julie, was born in 1948.) He made hundreds of speeches. In them he argued for free enterprise and against government regulation of the economy. He asserted that President Roosevelt had been lax in letting left-wingers into federal agencies. He contended that the United States should take a leading role in the United Nations, which had been formed just after the conclusion of the war. Above all, he argued that American labor unions were dominated by Communists.

Nixon's platform was the standard Republican line of the day. But Nixon made his case forcefully—and not always truthfully. He claimed that his opponent had been endorsed by the Congress of Industrial Organizations (CIO), a labor union that at the time had some leaders with ties to the Communist party. In fact, the CIO had not endorsed Voorhis, who was a liberal, not a Communist. Nixon blurred this distinction and encouraged voters to do the same thing. This situation gave Nixon an edge. He got more help from the backing of local newspapers that were owned by Republicans.

The candidates met in debate on September 13, 1946, in Pasadena, a wealthy suburb of Los Angeles that was predominantly Republican. Nearly a thousand people attended the debate, held in a junior high school auditorium. Voorhis spoke first, ranging over a variety of issues. When Nixon's turn came, he accused his opponent of having been endorsed by the Communist wing of the CIO. This untrue charge took Voorhis by surprise. He never recovered, during the debate or afterward, in the campaign. Nixon followed up with other attacks on Voorhis's character and career. When election day came in November, Nixon won by the large margin of 57 percent to 43. At age thirty-three he had been elected to the U.S. House of Representatives.

MAKING HEADLINES
The Nixons left for Washington in December 1946 and settled into a rented garden apartment in Virginia. On January 3, 1947, Richard Nixon was sworn in to the eightieth Congress. He was part of its Republican majority, the first the House had seen in sixteen years. There, like most other Republicans, Nixon voted for the passage of the Taft-Hartley Labor Act, which weakened the power of unions to strike against management. He voted in Congress against programs that Republicans had long opposed; programs begun under President Roosevelt that funded school lunches, that increased Social Security payments to the elderly, that built public housing and rural electrification systems, and so on.

Nixon was not strictly a "party man," however. For one thing, he differed with many conservatives on civil rights. He firmly believed in equal opportunity for minorities and consequently voted in favor of legislation that supported it. Nixon also differed with his party on foreign affairs. He backed aid to war-ravaged Europe and lobbied for passage of the Marshall Plan, devised by President Harry S Truman, the Democratic successor to Roosevelt, and by Secretary of State George C. Marshall, as a means of rebuilding the economies of the European nations.

Nixon's voting record made little impression on his colleagues or on the general public, but something else did. In fact, it made Nixon the best-known politician of his generation.

While serving his first term as congressman from California's twelfth district, Nixon presides briefly over the House of Representatives during a 1947 debate.

It all began with Nixon's role on the House Committee on Un-American Activities, known as HUAC. Since the late 1930s, the committee had been conducting investigations into allegedly subversive—"un-American"—activities that it saw as threatening the security of the United States. Communists were HUAC's prime target. The committee did turn up a few, but none seemed to present much of a threat. Then, on August 3, 1948, Whittaker Chambers, a senior editor at *Time* magazine, testified before HUAC in response to a summons. Chambers told the congressmen that he had been an underground member of the Communist party in the 1930s. He said his confederates there had included many government officials. One of them was, he said, Alger Hiss, a former official of the State Department who had helped organize the United Nations in 1945. Since 1947, Hiss had been president of the Carnegie Endowment for International Peace, a prestigious foundation in New York.

When Hiss heard of Chambers's charges, he demanded equal time before HUAC. He appeared two days after Chambers and denied everything Chambers had said. Hiss said he was not then a Communist and never had been one. He had no sympathy for Communists. And he said he could hardly have been Chambers's underground colleague, because "so far as I know, I have never laid eyes on" him.

The committee was stunned. They were used to "unfriendly" witnesses who refused to answer charges about their past connections with the Communist party. Here, however, was a man who met the accusations head on and flatly denied them. The situation was embarrassing to HUAC, and most members wanted to drop the inquiry—but not Richard Nixon. He had prior information that linked Hiss to the Communist party. Instead of telling his colleagues about this, he suggested that he form a HUAC subcommittee that would assume all responsibility for the investigation. Nixon then met with Chambers to find out just how much he knew about Hiss. The results were impressive. Chambers could remember details about Hiss's home and its furnishings. He knew the nicknames used by Hiss and his wife, Priscilla, and even their hobbies. All this convinced Nixon that on one key issue, at least, Chambers had told the truth and Hiss had lied: the two men had indeed known each other. At this point Nixon arranged a surprise meeting between accuser and accused. Hiss, caught off guard, finally admitted that he might have known Chambers in the 1930s after all. But Hiss said the relationship was not at all what Chambers claimed. According to Hiss, he had known Chambers by another name, George Crosley, and "Crosley" had told Hiss he was a freelance writer.

In September 1948, Hiss sued Chambers for libel. Hiss's lawyers called Chambers in for questioning. The defendant appeared with a stack of papers. Some were notes, written in Hiss's hand; others were typed documents. All dealt with State Department matters. Chambers said he had secretly received them from Hiss in 1938. A week later, HUAC investigators visited Chambers on his Maryland farm. He led them to a field where there were pumpkins. Picking one up, he pulled off its top. Inside, it had been hollowed out. Chambers reached in and removed several rolls of microfilm. They contained photographs of confidential documents, Chambers said, some of which had come from Alger Hiss.

All these twists and turns caused a sensation, with Nixon centrally involved. Newsreels showed the congressman skillfully questioning Chambers and Hiss. One photo showed Nixon peering intently through a magnifying glass at a strip of microfilm. On December 15, 1948, a grand jury in New York indicted Hiss on two counts of perjury—lying to the committee about whether or not he had known Chambers. Then there were two trials in 1949. The first reached no verdict, though eight out of twelve jurors thought Hiss guilty. The second perjury trial ended in his conviction, and in January 1950 Alger Hiss was sentenced to a five-year prison term.

And Richard Nixon was, at thirty-five, a celebrity.

AIMING HIGHER

Like any ambitious man, Nixon did not rest on his laurels. He now had a new goal: the Senate. In 1949, after winning easy reelection to the House of Representatives, he announced his candidacy for the Senate. California was an important state. To be one of its two senators would make him powerful indeed.

His Democratic opponent was Helen Gahagan Douglas. She was fifty, a member of Congress, and a former actress (her husband, Melvyn Douglas, was a Hollywood star). She was also a liberal. "I welcome Mrs. Douglas as an opponent," Nixon said. He promised that "it won't be a campaign of personalities, but of issues." The issues were again the ones Nixon had stressed when he had run for the House in 1946. Nixon attacked what he called Douglas's "soft attitude toward Communism." He circulated a document that listed occasions on which Douglas had voted the same way as, in Nixon's words, "the notorious Communist Party-liner, Congressman Vito Marcantonio." This was misleading, to say the least. None of these votes were enough to prove that Douglas herself was a Communist, and there were some bills on which even the most conservative Republicans had voted the same way as Marcantonio. However, the damage had been done.

Nixon's Senate campaign was superior to his opponent's—better financed, better organized, and better managed. He won the support of most California newspapers, which slanted their coverage to favor him. And his radio advertisements included slogans such as "Fight the Red fear with a fearless man—Dick Nixon" and "Be an American, Vote for Nixon." On election day, November 1950, helicopters dropped leaflets that read, "Every Communist who goes to the polls will vote against Nixon and for Mrs. Douglas. Which way will you vote?"

Douglas fought back. "They are trying to scare you," she told one crowd. "I despise Communism, Nazism, and Nixonism." She claimed, "I would rather be right than Senator." She got her wish. Nixon trounced her, 59 percent to 40, the biggest landslide in the Senate election that year. In four years, Nixon had risen from obscurity to join "the most exclusive club in America."

3

ON THE NATIONAL TICKET

Richard Nixon's career in the Senate was similar to his career in the House. He continued to denounce Communists and what he saw as their influence in government. He strongly supported foreign aid and backed America's Western allies. Again he voted with his party on most domestic issues, but broke with it on civil rights measures. For example, Nixon sided with the liberals by voting for a civil rights bill prohibiting the poll tax—a fee for voting that some states charged that discriminated against poor black and white voters.

WINNING STRATEGIES
The day-to-day business of the Senate did not much interest Nixon. He had his eye on another job, the vice-presidency of the United States. In 1952 the Republicans had a good chance to win the White House. Nixon was not ready for the top slot, but he knew he was an attractive choice to fill out the ticket. He was young (thirty-nine in 1952), a skillful campaigner, and he was a recognized name. He was also from the West. This meant he could "balance the ticket" if the presidential nominee came from the East or the Midwest.

There were two obstacles in his path, however. The first was Earl Warren, the popular governor of California and the choice of some Republicans to run for president. Should he win, he would need to look outside his own state for a running mate. Another front-runner, Senator Robert Taft, was from Ohio. He had already expressed a vice-presidential preference, however—the senior senator from California, William Knowland. Nixon's hope lay with the third candidate, Dwight D. Eisenhower. "Ike," as he was universally known, had led the Allies to victory in World War II. He had since served as president of Columbia University and as Supreme Commander of the North Atlantic Treaty Organization (NATO).

Nixon and Eisenhower first met in May 1951. Each came away favorably impressed. The general complimented Nixon on his work in the Hiss case. The senator said he considered Ike a great world leader and a shoo-in for the presidency. But first the field had to be cleared of Taft and Warren.

In July 1952 the Republican party convened in Chicago to choose a presidential nominee. Taft had an edge, because he had won more delegates in the primaries held that spring. Eisenhower's aides objected, though. They said that from some states their man's delegates, and not Taft's, should be seated. They called for a vote on which delegates to admit to the convention and proposed that the contested delegates be barred from the voting. This procedural change would shift the advantage to Eisenhower.

Nixon arrived in Chicago as a delegate from California. He was pledged not to Eisenhower but to Earl Warren, for good reason. Early in the campaign, Nixon had guessed that it would take some doing for Eisenhower to get the nomination. Ever the shrewd tactician, Nixon had a plan. Instead of simply declaring himself for Eisenhower, he had joined California Republicans calling for Warren to run. Nixon's reward was to be made a delegate to the convention and, further, to be given the right to choose twenty-three other California delegates out of the seventy-person total. Warren then bested Taft in the California primary, and Nixon and his hand-picked slate qualified as delegates for the Chicago convention. This was his situation when the Eisenhower–Taft fight came up.

Nixon now went to work. He told the California delegation that Warren had no chance of winning the nomination, that Ike did, and that California could make the difference. For this reason, he said, they should desert Warren, as he planned to do, and back Eisenhower. Warren was irate—his own man was undercutting his candidacy—but it was too late. Nixon had outfoxed him. The California delegates supported Eisenhower, who went on to capture the nomination.

Nixon's ingenuity in securing Eisenhower's nomination was not lost on the nominee and his aides. So skillful an infighter could only help in the presidential race. Eisenhower's staff asked Nixon if he was interested in the vice-presidency, and on July 11, 1952, Richard Nixon was nominated by the convention. Nixon later maintained that he had viewed himself as a long shot. "I did not think I had more than a remote chance to be nominated," he wrote in his memoir, *Six Crises*. "I had not even bothered to pack a dark suit for the trip."

THE "CHECKERS" SPEECH

Nixon entered the 1952 campaign as an asset to the ticket. Two months later he had become a liability. It happened this way. In 1950, Dana Smith, a Nixon backer from southern

California, had set up a bank account for the new senator from California. Smith encouraged other well-heeled supporters to contribute to it, with the idea that the extra money would help Nixon—who was not well-to-do—meet his expenses. The ceiling for donations was $500, the average $240. The total collected was about $18,000. All but $66 had been spent by September 1952, when news of this secret fund surfaced.

It surfaced loudly, because such a fund was illegal. The contributions to it had not been recorded, as required by law. Also, the amount of money in the fund exceeded Nixon's salary. In effect, he was being paid more by his backers than by his own government, which could have compromised his integrity. On September 18, 1952, the story of this fund was sent to hundreds of newspapers. "Secret Rich Men's Trust Fund Keeps Nixon in Style Far Beyond His Salary" read a headline in the *New York Post.* A California daily, the *Sacramento Bee,* published an editorial calling Nixon "a subsidized front man" and a "lobbyist" for rich Californians. Stephen Mitchell, the chairman of the Democratic National Committee, called for Nixon to withdraw from the ticket.

Nixon hit back hard in a statement that denounced the "smear tactics" of "left-wingers, fellow travelers, and former Communists." In fact, it was California Republicans, angry about Nixon's betrayal of Earl Warren, who had released the story about the fund. Nixon issued another statement, justifying the fund by saying it was used only to meet travel expenses. But this explanation would not do, either. If his travel costs were indeed high, there was public money available to cover them.

Eisenhower's aides were distraught. The campaign was in deep water. "Let's find out the facts before I shoot my mouth off," said Eisenhower. He sent a telegram to Nixon advising him to publish a full account of the fund. Nixon telegramed back that the secret contributors received no "special favors, consideration, or treatment." Eisenhower's staff was divided about Nixon. Some wanted him dropped from the ticket; others were uncertain. Meanwhile, the *Washington Post* and the *New York Herald-Tribune* called for Nixon to withdraw. Nixon regarded the New York paper as being close to Eisenhower and interpreted its view as a reflection of Ike's own. But Eisenhower himself had not yet made up his mind.

Nixon's staff wanted to seize the initiative. "Every time you get before an audience," said his campaign manager, Murray Chotiner, "you win them. What we have to do is get you before the biggest possible audience so that you can talk over the heads of the press to the people." Nixon decided to go on television, and Eisenhower approved. "Tell them everything there is to tell," Ike advised his running mate, who quoted his words in *Six Crises,* "everything that you can remember since the day you entered public life."

This was a tall order. Nixon had a lot of explaining to do. He would have to comment not only on this first secret fund but also on another, begun after his nomination for the vice-presidency. He would have to explain why, if the fund had not entitled contributors to special favors, his votes in the Senate had coincided more than once with the wishes of contributors with banking and dairy interests. He would also have to explain how, if the $18,000 had in fact gone toward his traveling expenses, he had been able to purchase a new home. The Republican National Committee bought air time for the candidate, and more than sixty television stations and over seven hundred radio stations agreed to carry the special broadcast. "I knew I had to go for broke," Nixon wrote in

Six Crises. "I had to launch a political counterattack." Nixon's resolve stiffened when he learned that Eisenhower's advisors wanted him to resign at the conclusion of his talk.

At NBC's El Capitan television studio, Nixon mounted a stage designed to resemble a den in an ordinary, middle-class American home. The red camera light flashed on, and Nixon read from the speech he had prepared. He had not used the secret fund, he said, to meet personal expenses. No contribu-

The Nixon family vacationing at the Jersey shore with their dog Checkers. Tricia Nixon, age seven, holds some seaweed; Julie, five, holds her father's hand.

tor had received special consideration. Next Nixon cited—and exaggerated—his war record. Then he brought in his family. Pat, he said (as the camera panned to his wife), did not wear fancy clothes but "a respectable Republican cloth coat." Yes, Nixon admitted, he had accepted one gift from a supporter: someone had once given his two daughters a cocker spaniel, which they had named Checkers. "And you know the kids love the dog and I just want to say this right now, that regardless of what they say about it, we're going to keep it."

Nixon then shifted to counterattack. He called for the Democratic nominees—Governor Adlai Stevenson of Illinois and his running mate, Senator John Sparkman of Alabama—to make a complete financial statement. He finished with a thrust at Eisenhower's camp. Instead of offering to resign he invited his listeners to contact the Republican National Committee and express their opinion as to whether he should quit the race or stay in it. This took an immediate decision out of the hands of Eisenhower's aides—the general himself had not asked Nixon to resign—and placed it in the hands of the National Committee, where Nixon had supporters.

This "Checkers" speech was a smash hit. Public opinion now swung toward Nixon. Telegrams ran 100 to 1 in his favor. "They not only want you to remain on the ticket," the candidate learned the next day from the Republican National Committee, "they demand it."

Nixon stayed on the ticket, and the Republicans won control of the White House for the first time since 1928. Nixon, at thirty-nine, had been elected vice-president of the United States.

4

A Heartbeat Away

"My country has in its wisdom contrived for me the most insignificant office that ever the invention of man contrived or his imagination conceived," complained John Adams, the first vice-president, in the eighteenth century. Not much had changed by 1953 when Richard Nixon was sworn into the same office. But with his enormous energy and political skills, Nixon created the modern conception of the vice-presidency. For instance, he was the first in that office to take advantage of rapid air travel and mass communication. Doing so enabled him to build support within the Republican party and to create his own public image.

GLOBE-TROTTING

Nixon was often on the road, or in the air. As vice-president he made seven different international trips, which took him to fifty-four countries and every continent but Antarctica. His first global venture came in 1953, a seventy-two-day trip to the Far East. His purpose there was to explain America's peace policy in Korea. In 1956 he went on Operation Mercy, a trip to Austria intended to draw the attention of Americans to the plight of refugees fleeing from Hungary after the Soviet

Union's invasion of their country. Nixon toured Africa in 1957 and England in 1958. On this last visit he was especially popular.

In the fall of 1958 he made a more eventful trip, to Latin America. Nixon was received cordially in Argentina, Uruguay, Ecuador, and Colombia. Then he proceeded to Lima, the capital of Peru. There, at San Marcos University, student demonstrators shouted, "Fuera Nixon!" ("Nixon, go home!") Fifty yards from the university's main gate Nixon stopped the motorcade, climbed out of his car, and approached the students, who began hurling stones, forcing him back to his car. As the motorcade pulled away, Nixon shouted at the students, "You are cowards, you are afraid of the truth!" At his hotel another mob awaited Nixon. One of the demonstrators there spat in his face. "I at least had the satisfaction," Nixon remarked in *Six Crises,* "of planting a healthy kick on his shins. Nothing I did all day made me feel better."

Things only got worse in Venezuela, where the citizens were outraged that the United States had granted asylum to their ousted dictator. A mob formed a blockade and attacked Nixon's car with rocks and pipes, smashing the windshield. Bits of glass injured one eye of the Venezuelan foreign minister, who was riding with Nixon. The vice-president was hit in the face. The mob shouted, "Muera Nixon, Muera Nixon!" ("Death to Nixon!") The driver of the car finally delivered his cargo to safety. President Eisenhower ordered American troops to nearby bases in case the Nixons had to be rescued.

The next year, Nixon had a more rewarding foreign adventure when he went to the Soviet Union to open the American exhibition at Sokolniki Park in Moscow. His host

Vice-President Nixon with Soviet leader Nikita Khrushchev at the opening of an exhibit of American consumer products at a Moscow trade fair. The Soviets could not believe that American workers could buy the kitchen products on display.

was Nikita Khrushchev, the Soviet premier. Together the two men attended the exhibition and stopped at a full-sized model of an American house. Nixon told his host that this was just the sort of house an American steelworker might live in. Because it was much better furnished than the house a Soviet worker was likely to live in, the implied comparison irked Khrushchev, who began to shout at his guest. "Your generals say we must compete in rockets. Your generals say they are so powerful they can destroy us. We can also show you something so that you know the Russian spirit. We are strong. We can beat you." Nixon was taken aback, but he responded diplomatically. "For us to argue who is the stronger misses the point. If war comes, we both lose." Khrushchev would not be placated. He shouted again, "We too are giants. You want to threaten—we will answer threats with threats." Nixon held his ground, and Khrushchev gradually became friendlier. "We want peace and friendship with all nations," he said, "especially with America." Nixon echoed this sentiment. This "kitchen debate," as it came to be known, was widely reported in the United States and won Nixon points for going head to head with the tough-talking leader of the Soviet Union.

Nixon's Soviet visit concluded with his taking to the airwaves to address the Russian people, the first American leader to do so. Nixon told the Soviets that the United States was a peaceful and tolerant nation. "The very essence of our belief is that we do not and will not try to impose our system on anybody else. We believe that you and all other peoples on this earth should have the right to choose the kind of economic or political system which best fits your particular problems, without any foreign intervention."

THE HEARTBEAT QUICKENS

On Saturday, September 24, 1955, the Nixon family was relaxing at home after attending a wedding. The afternoon calm was interrupted by a telephone call from the White House press secretary, Jim Hagerty. "The President," Hagerty told Nixon, "has had a coronary." Eisenhower had been vacationing in Denver, Colorado. There he had suffered a heart attack after playing twenty-seven holes of golf, just twenty days shy of his sixty-fifth birthday.

Nixon reacted decisively. He conferred with Attorney General William Rogers and the two worked out a plan. As long as the emergency lasted, a team was to handle the daily business of the administration. Secretary of State John Foster Dulles would take the senior role in the cabinet. White House chief of staff Sherman Adams would fly to Denver. There he would remain at the president's side and serve as intermediary between Ike and the cabinet. What role would Nixon play? In *Six Crises* he described it this way: "My own position as Vice President called for maintaining a balance of the utmost delicacy." There could not be "any move on my part which could be interpreted, even incorrectly, as an attempt to usurp the powers of the presidency." He saw his task as being "to provide leadership without appearing to lead."

While Eisenhower was recovering, Nixon chaired nineteen cabinet meetings and twenty-six sessions of the National Security Council. He made it clear, however, that he was not pretending to be president. "I sat in the Vice President's chair, opposite the President's, and I was careful to act more as moderator than director," he later wrote. Nixon took other precautions. He continued to work in the Senate Office Building, not the White House. He visited cabinet members in their offices rather than having them visit his. When Eisenhower finally resumed his duties in November, observers agreed that Nixon had handled the situation with tact and skill.

"DUMP NIXON"

Nixon was a favorite of Republican party regulars, meaning those who influenced the policies and direction of the party. But outside its ranks "Tricky Dick," as some called him, had many enemies. They detested his campaign style, with its smears and name calling. The private fund scandal of 1952 had further tarnished his reputation. There were many Democratic voters who approved of the job that Eisenhower had done and might desert their party to vote for him—but would not do so if Nixon remained on the ticket. As the date of the Republican nomination neared, there was a movement afoot to "dump Nixon."

It was not clear where Eisenhower himself stood, and a meeting Nixon had with him only confused matters. On that occasion the president said that Nixon, who was then only forty-three, should consider leaving the vice-presidency for a cabinet post. He could thus get out from under Eisenhower's shadow. But was this sound advice? It was no secret that Nixon hoped to become president someday. As vice-president he stood in line for the Republican nomination. If he were pushed into the cabinet it might seem that Eisenhower was sending the message that Nixon was not, as the vice-president's opponents were already saying, "presidential material."

Ever the shrewd tactician, Nixon gave the matter some thought. He met again with Eisenhower. This time, Nixon put the ball in Eisenhower's court, as he later wrote in *Six*

The Republican National Convention renominated Vice-President Nixon for a second term in 1956, after Nixon had survived attempts by some Republican politicians to dump him from the national ticket.

Crises. "If you believe your own candidacy and your administration would be better served with me off the ticket," Nixon told the president, "you tell me what you want me to do and I'll do it." Ike would not be pinned down. "No," he replied, "I think we've got to do what's best for you." Even more pressure was put on Nixon when John Foster Dulles confided that he was thinking of resigning his post as secretary of state and that Eisenhower was willing to give the job to Nixon.

On February 29, 1956, Eisenhower announced that he would seek a second term. Reporters asked if Nixon would be on the ticket. The decision, said the president, was up to the party. This came as hardly an endorsement. At another press conference, Eisenhower said that it was up to Nixon to "chart out his own course." He seemed to be waiting for Nixon to bow out. Nixon's backers moved swiftly to help their man. During the first primary, in New Hampshire, they organized a write-in vote supporting Nixon as vice-president. The response was both favorable and strong. On April 26, Nixon paid a call on the president to inform his chief that he had indeed "charted out his own course." He wanted to stay on the ticket. Eisenhower had no choice but to accept this decision.

On August 22, the Republican party renominated Eisenhower and Nixon. Then in November the team swept to victory with 60 percent of the vote. Nixon, as always, campaigned effectively, not only for himself but for other Republicans who were up for election that year. This record of service to his party later made Nixon the logical choice for the presidential nomination, in 1960.

5

Hard Losses

The best way to become president is first to be vice-president. In all, thirteen vice-presidents have subsequently reached the higher office. Nine did so after the death or resignation of the incumbent, and four won their own elections. Since 1960 every vice-president who has sought the presidential nomination of his party has captured it—Nixon in 1960, Hubert Humphrey in 1968, Walter Mondale in 1984, and George Bush in 1988.

STRATEGY
Richard Nixon gathered support by campaigning hard for Republican congressional candidates who ran in 1958. However, the outcome was disastrous. Republicans elected only 35 senators out of 100, 153 members of the House out of 435, and 14 governors out of 50. Eisenhower himself was still popular, but voters seemed eager for a large-scale change in those in government. In a trial heat held in 1958 between Nixon and Senator John F. Kennedy, Democrat of Massachusetts, pollsters put Kennedy ahead, 59 percent to 41. Nixon had a strong chance of winning his own party's nomination, but the party itself was in a weak position. To gain the White

House Nixon would have to win the nomination in a way that appealed both to independent voters and even to some Democrats.

In January 1959 Nixon met with advisors in Key Biscayne, Florida, to develop a campaign strategy. He had a clear enough path to the nomination. But, as he wrote in *Six Crises,* "the problem was to win it in such a way as to strengthen rather than weaken our chances to win the November election." Nixon had to present himself as a progressive, not a conservative, if he hoped to collect the needed 5 to 6 million Democratic votes that would win him the election. In keeping with this strategy, Nixon indicated that his choice for vice-president was Nelson Rockefeller, the highly popular governor of New York and a liberal Republican. It turned out that Rockefeller was not interested, though. He told reporters that he was not even planning to attend the party's convention.

THE PLATFORM FIGHT

In May 1960 Nixon's nomination suffered a curious setback. An American spy plane flying secretly over the Soviet Union was shot down by a Soviet missile. The pilot, Francis Gary Powers, was carrying with him a poison capsule. The Eisenhower administration, which had assumed that Powers had swallowed the poison, denied that a spy plane had violated Soviet air space. At that point Nikita Khrushchev produced Powers for the world to see. When the Soviet leader met Eisenhower in Paris for a summit meeting, Khrushchev called his American counterpart a liar, then broke up the meeting.

Rockefeller, who had been laying low, now sprang into action. On June 8 he announced his candidacy for the presidential nomination. "A new period now begins," he said. "It summons new men. New problems demand new ideas, new actions." He then presented a nine-point program that repudiated many policies of the Eisenhower administration. He also set forth his own ideas for the Republican party's platform. This initiative posed a direct challenge to Nixon, who had chaired the Republican Committee on Program and Progress. This committee oversaw a Republican platform that praised the Eisenhower record. Before the nominating convention met, Rockefeller's forces narrowed their focus to two main issues: defense policy and civil rights.

"My most critical problem," Nixon wrote in *Six Crises,* "was to see that our Convention ended with all Republicans united behind the ticket." Nixon could have defeated the Rockefeller camp's platform proposals as they came up to be voted on at the convention. Instead he compromised, for the sake of party unity. On June 22, Nixon went to Rockefeller's New York apartment and drafted with him a compromise document known as the Fourteen Point Compact of Fifth Avenue. On most points the vice-president yielded to the governor. The Republican Committee was outraged. "I found the delegates in an angry and rebellious mood," Nixon recounted in his memoirs. President Eisenhower was also angry—because the compact implicitly repudiated his record. According to Theodore White in *The Making of the President: 1960,* Senator Barry Goldwater of Arizona, the leading Republican conservative, said that the agreement would lead to "a Republican defeat in November." The platform committee therefore rejected the Nixon–Rockefeller compact and released its own statement.

Nixon's deal with Rockefeller did help him in one crucial respect. It put him at odds with the right wing of his own party and so established him—to the wider public, Democrats included—as a moderate. It also freed him from his alliance with Eisenhower. When Nixon got to Chicago, he fought for the Nixon–Rockefeller plank on civil rights, in opposition to the party's wishes. "We collected every political IOU we held in the country that night," White quotes one of Nixon's aides as saying. Nixon buttonholed each member of the platform committee and insisted that the language be changed. Then he fashioned a compromise between the Rockefeller and Eisenhower positions on national defense.

On July 27, 1960, Richard M. Nixon became his party's nominee for president of the United States. His choice for vice-president was Henry Cabot Lodge, ambassador to the United Nations in the Eisenhower administration.

OVERDOING IT

Nixon now had to win the general election, which would be a close race. Senator John F. Kennedy was a formidable opponent—handsome, charming, intelligent, and popular. Nixon's plan was to emphasize his own superior experience. Kennedy was younger than he was by four years, and had not achieved much as a legislator. Nixon wanted to appear to be the calm statesman—until the last few weeks of the campaign. At this point he would use a media "blitz." This way he would avoid "peaking" too early. The proper timing was thus essential.

The night he was nominated, Nixon pledged to campaign "in every one of the fifty states between now and November eighth." This was a rash promise. His staff calculated that the election would be decided in the largest industrial states that had the most electoral votes: California, New York, Illinois, Ohio, Pennsylvania, Texas, and Michigan. In all likelihood,

Nixon would need to spend most of his time in them. Around Labor Day, Nixon injured a knee. It became infected, so that he had to be hospitalized for more than a week. This cost him valuable time. Then he worked so hard to catch up that he came down with several colds and a fever. He lost weight and grew haggard and hoarse. His campaign pledge now came back to haunt him. He had to travel to states that were already won or lost, when what he should have been doing was making last stops in states that were still undecided. On the final weekend of the campaign he found himself in Alaska, rather than in the key industrial regions.

This was not Nixon's only campaign mistake. Some of his other decisions were equally confused, such as his southern strategy. At first he simply conceded the southern states, which were traditionally Democratic, and focused instead on the North, where his strong civil rights plank should have won him votes. But then he realized that Kennedy would likely lose votes in the South because some of its heavily Protestant population was prejudiced against Kennedy as a Catholic. Nixon himself did not comment on his opponent's religion. He thought it would be inappropriate and a tactical mistake. At the same time, however, he knew that Kennedy's religion would alienate some Southerners and dispose them to vote for himself—but only if Nixon moderated his own stand on civil rights and disavowed a pledge by his running mate to appoint a black to a cabinet position. This he did—and thereby disturbed many black voters in the North. Nixon in fact outwitted himself. In the end Kennedy took the South, thanks in large part to his running mate, Senator Lyndon Baines Johnson of Texas.

Nixon's worst strategic error was overconfidence. He was convinced he was simply a better candidate than Kennedy.

When the television networks offered free time for a series of debates between the candidates, Nixon was certain he would thrash his opponent. They had indeed crossed swords once before, in 1947, when both were freshmen congressmen. They had debated then on a labor question, and Nixon had come out on top.

This time the two candidates agreed to a set of four debates, the first to be held on September 26. The two opponents took completely different approaches to preparing for the debates. Kennedy rehearsed answers to hypothetical questions and memorized material prepared by his advisors; Nixon hastily crammed on the last day. Kennedy relaxed before the first contest by chatting in his hotel room with friends; Nixon spent the day alone. Kennedy looked tanned and relaxed, the

Richard Nixon debated John F. Kennedy in the first televised debates between two presidential candidates in the nation's history. More than 100 million viewers watched the first debate, and the majority believed that Kennedy won.

picture of health. Nixon was ill and exhausted from his heavy campaign schedule. Kennedy asked to be briefed on the entire setup of the studio. Nixon sat still only for a ten-minute rundown on the ride to the studio. Kennedy stepped before the camera dressed in a dark blue suit that presented a crisp contrast to the studio's backdrop. Nixon's bland gray suit instead emphasized his pasty complexion. Kennedy wore the proper television makeup, but Nixon would not allow it. Instead he used Lazy Shave, a pancake powder that was supposed to conceal his "five o'clock shadow."

The radio listeners thought the first debate was a draw. But a large majority of the television viewers—all told there were some 80 million—believed that Kennedy had won. As described by Theodore White, "Probably no picture in American politics tells a better story than that famous shot of the camera on the Vice President as he half slouched, his 'Lazy Shave' powder faintly streaked with sweat, his eyes exaggerated hollows of blackness, his jaw, jowls, and face drooping with strain." In the three other debates Nixon recovered and did well, but the damage had been done. Kennedy had shown the public that he was at least Nixon's equal.

The last weeks of the campaign passed in a whirl of feverish activity. Gallup polls showed a 50–50 split at Labor Day and a 51–49 percent Kennedy lead in mid-September. Some of Nixon's advisors suggested he make an issue of Kennedy's Catholicism, but Nixon declined. He focused instead on economics and foreign policy. He asserted that Kennedy's program would raise prices by 25 percent and charged that Kennedy was not tough enough to stand up to the Russians.

Nixon started to gain on his opponent. For one thing, farmers in the Midwest were not impressed by Kennedy's agricultural program. And President Eisenhower, whose absence from the campaign had embarrassed Nixon, finally made appearances in Pittsburgh, Cleveland, and New York, where Kennedy held the advantage.

MISSING BY A WHISKER

The campaign was finally over. Nixon had flown 65,000 miles, stopped in 188 cities, made more than 150 speeches, and had indeed visited, as promised, all fifty states. On the last day he flew into Los Angeles, where he was welcomed by a crowd of fifteen thousand. All that remained was to await the verdict of the 68,832,818 Americans who would vote. Nixon jumped off to an early lead: the Associated Press tabulation of the initial voting figures showed 203,628 for Nixon, with only 166,963 for Kennedy. At 7:15 P.M., CBS News made the first computerized analysis of voting returns in American history, which gave Nixon odds of 500 to 1. The network predicted an electoral-vote margin for Nixon of 459 to 78, a landslide.

Then the momentum shifted. At 8:00 P.M. the computer gave Kennedy 51 percent of the vote. Next he took Connecticut, a swing state that Nixon had hoped would go his way. By 10:30 P.M. Kennedy had swept Pennsylvania, New York, Rhode Island, Massachusetts, and Maryland and was holding on, though by only razor-thin margins, in every southern state except Virginia and Florida. The NBC computer predicted that Kennedy would win with 401 electoral college votes. Nixon was looking strong in Kentucky, Oklahoma, Indiana, Iowa, Michigan, Ohio, and even Wisconsin, which Kennedy had hoped to carry. The Rocky Mountain states all went for Nixon, by large majorities.

By midnight, both camps realized that the election would be decided by only a very few states: Michigan, Minnesota,

Illinois, and California. Nixon needed all four of them, but Kennedy needed only two—any two. If he took only one, then fourteen members of the electoral college from the South could either decide the election or force the contest into being decided by a vote in the House of Representatives.

As dawn broke, it became clear that Michigan had gone for Kennedy. Therefore, Nixon could not win. Then, at 9:30 A.M. (Pacific time), California went to Kennedy. Secret Service men moved onto the grounds of Kennedy's house to establish security for the now president-elect. It had been ever so close. "You know Dick," his campaign manager Len Hall said later. "A switch of only fourteen thousand votes and we would have been the heroes and they would have been the bums." Others urged Nixon to challenge the returns in Illinois and Texas, where there had been widespread rumors of fraud. Nixon refused to do this, however. One reason was that a recount could take as long as a year and a half, which might throw the nation into chaos. A recount would also likely undermine public confidence in the electoral process. Nixon decided he did not want the presidency on those terms.

Ironically, it fell to Richard Nixon, as presiding officer of the Senate, to formally announce that John F. Kennedy had been elected president of the United States. The margin was 303 electoral votes to 219. (Fifteen southern electoral votes had been pledged to neither candidate, but cast for a southern senator, Harry Byrd of Virginia.) After Nixon made the announcement, he received a standing ovation, from Democrats as well as Republicans.

On January 20, 1961, as the Kennedy administration assumed power, Richard and Pat Nixon attended a farewell luncheon for the Eisenhowers. That evening, Nixon had his chauffeur take him for a final vice-presidential visit to Capitol

Hill, as the car and driver would be relinquished the next day. Nixon stepped out and climbed up the steps and into the building. As he walked outside onto the balcony and stared out over the Mall it was chilly, so he did not stay long. "As I turned to go inside, I suddenly stopped short," he later recounted, "struck by the thought that this was not the end—that someday I would be back here."

A PAINFUL FAREWELL

In *Six Crises,* Nixon describes a conversation he had with his daughter Julie after his presidential defeat in 1960. "What are we going to do?" Julie then asked. "Where are we going to live? What kind of a job are you going to be able to get? Where are we going to school?" These were serious questions—Nixon was at a crossroads. He decided to move back to California and resume the practice of law, not in Whittier again but with the large Los Angeles firm of Adams, Duque and Hazeltine. Pat Nixon stayed on in Washington until Julie and Tricia could finish out the semester at the high school they were attending. In Los Angeles, Nixon rented a small bachelor apartment and learned to cook, or at least to heat up TV dinners.

Meanwhile, Nixon's friends were urging him to run against the incumbent Edmund "Pat" Brown for governor of California. Eisenhower concurred, saying he thought Nixon could use the governorship to mount another run for the White House, in 1964. Whittaker Chambers, who had by now become a highly influential conservative writer, wrote to Nixon, urging him to run. The polls predicted Nixon would trounce Brown. Others believed that Nixon should run again for the Senate, where he could concentrate on international affairs. Nixon himself had no wish to be governor, and Pat was dead set against it. "If you run this time," she told him, "I'm not going to be out campaigning with you as I have in the past."

In the end, the lure of campaigning proved too strong to resist. Nixon entered the Republican gubernatorial primary and swept to victory, though some right-wingers deserted him because he refused to accept the endorsement of the John Birch Society. It was a California fringe group whose founder had called Eisenhower "a dedicated, conscious agent of the Communist conspiracy" and John Foster Dulles "a Communist agent." A bigger problem was that Nixon could not convince voters that he was sincerely interested in the job. Two-thirds of them believed that he was in the race only as a stepping stone to the presidency. When Nixon lost to Governor Brown by almost 300,000 votes out of a total of 6 million it was a humiliating defeat for a man who had nearly captured the presidency just two years earlier.

After this loss, reporters waited for Nixon to speak with them. "I'm not going to do it," he told his press secretary. "I don't have to, and I'm not going to." But at last he did. "Good morning, gentlemen," Nixon began, addressing the room full of journalists. "Now that all the members of the press are so delighted that I have lost, I'd like to make a statement of my own." He told the reporters that he hoped they'd "give my opponent the same going over that you give me." He continued bitterly, "As I leave you I want you to know—just think of how much you're going to be missing. You won't have Nixon to kick around anymore, because, gentlemen, this is my last press conference." Then he concluded by urging the media to report all the news about a candidate and to "put one lonely reporter on the campaign who will report what the candidate says now and then. Thank you, gentlemen, and good day."

The media response came quickly. The Sunday evening after the election, an ABC television special was entitled "The Political Obituary of Richard Nixon."

6

THE ROAD TO THE WHITE HOUSE

Nixon was not yet fifty years old, and he had many options. The one he chose was to pursue the dream that had eluded him a quarter-century before. He moved to New York City and joined the large law firm of Mudge, Rose, Guthrie and Alexander and had his name duly placed at the head of the roster. For the first time, Nixon earned a truly large income, more than $250,000 per year (roughly the equivalent of $1 million today). This money was well earned. The former vice-president landed important clients and put his international experience to profitable use.

This job also gave a boost to his political fortunes, for Richard Nixon had no intention of leaving politics. His work gave him many opportunities to travel, and wherever he went he was news. In his first year out of office, he held more than fifty press conferences. As soon as Nixon left politics, he began to plan a comeback, despite what he had said at his "last" press conference.

Nixon did not enter the field, however, during the presidential election of 1964, although he was still the favorite among Republicans. He held off, for several good reasons. For one thing, his wife opposed entering into another grueling round of campaign stops. For another, the incumbent, John F. Kennedy, looked hard to beat. Then, on November 22, 1963, Kennedy was assassinated in Dallas, Texas. In addition to its other consequences, this catastrophe threw the upcoming 1964 election into chaos. The Republicans not only had to defeat Lyndon B. Johnson, who had succeeded to the White House upon Kennedy's death. The Republicans also had to run against the memory of a slain hero.

The Republican contest shaped up as a race between a conservative, Barry Goldwater, a senator from Arizona, and a liberal, Nelson Rockefeller, the governor of New York. Each represented a different faction of the party. The moderate Nixon tried to bind the Republicans together. He urged Rockefeller's supporters to help put Goldwater in office, but the nominee had other ideas. In his acceptance speech, Goldwater warned that "those who do not care for our cause we do not expect to enter our ranks." This and other remarks frightened off many Republicans. Some party leaders refused to endorse Goldwater. Many of the rank and file voted for Johnson. Goldwater won only 39 percent of the vote during the general election, one of the worst defeats in presidential campaign history.

THE MIDTERM CONGRESSIONAL ELECTIONS OF 1966

Perhaps surprisingly, Goldwater's loss actually helped Nixon. The fact that he had endorsed the nominee and tried to unify the party satisfied conservatives. At the same time, Nixon could now argue more forcefully than ever that only a moderate Republican had a chance to win the presidency. "Extremism," he warned, "will destroy freedom because it will destroy the world."

Nixon now reclaimed a role for himself in party affairs. His opportunity came with the 1966 congressional midterm elections. Nixon stumped tirelessly for his fellow Republicans. In 1965 he spoke to more than four hundred party organizations to raise money, and he campaigned for 105 congressional candidates in 1966. Nixon chose districts that were reliably Republican but had elected Democrats in the 1964 election. If these voters returned to Republican form, Nixon would be able to take some share of the credit.

As always, Nixon emphasized foreign affairs, especially President Johnson's military policies regarding Vietnam. Nixon wanted more American troops sent there and called for bombing North Vietnam, the Communist country that was threatening to overrun South Vietnam, an American ally. Many conservatives agreed with him. A group of business executives raised money and provided Nixon with a private jet for his campaign travels. Two days before the 1966 elections, Nixon appeared on national network talk shows, then on a half-hour election special paid for by the Republican National Committee. The Republicans did well. They gained 47 seats in the House and 3 in the Senate. And they won 8 new governorships and 540 state legislative seats. Nixon, who had a lot to do with that success, emerged as a strong contender for the 1968 nomination. Pat Nixon even overcame her distaste for political campaigns. She seated herself at a desk in her husband's law firm and, using her maiden name, Miss Ryan, helped Nixon's secretary, Rosemary Woods, keep up with Nixon's political correspondence.

A SECOND CHANCE

"My biggest problem is 'Nixon can't win,'" the candidate explained to his backers. The last election he had won in his own right had been in 1950, against a weak opponent, Helen Gahagan Douglas. His vice-presidential victories had both been on Eisenhower's coattails. Since then, running on his own, Nixon had lost to Kennedy in 1960 and Pat Brown in 1962. Nixon now had to convince convention delegates that he was a winner. In order to do this he had to run in the Republican primaries against other potential nominees. Several had come forward: Nelson Rockefeller again, Michigan governor George Romney, Illinois senator Charles Percy, and California governor Ronald Reagan. Nixon was confident that he would do well in the primaries and even better with the delegates chosen by state parties, thanks to all the campaigning and fundraising he had done for them over the years. He estimated that he would go into the convention, in Miami, with approximately 600 of the 667 delegate votes needed to secure the nomination.

Nixon was by now a seasoned campaigner. He had learned lessons from defeat, which he now put into practice. This time he slowed down the pace. And instead of seeking out individual voters on the streets, he addressed large audiences, to provide maximum television exposure. This technique helped him control the media coverage he received. Nixon also kept individual reporters at bay and fed them just one story each day, always one that highlighted a theme of his own choosing.

This strategy worked. Nixon shot up in the polls. One of his competitors, Governor Romney, sank so low that he withdrew himself from the race. On March 12, Nixon triumphed in the New Hampshire primary with 79 percent of the vote, a huge margin that solved the "Nixon can't win" problem. Nixon's delegate count at this point showed him with 725 pledged or "leaning" delegates, more than enough to secure the nomination. It was then sealed by the Oregon primary. There Nixon won a whopping 73 percent of the vote, versus 23 percent for Reagan and only 4 percent for Rockefeller. "The chances of my being derailed," Nixon said in his victory statement, "are pretty well eliminated." His only real concern was Reagan, who had inherited many of Barry Goldwater's supporters. Nixon met that challenge by landing the endorsement of Senator Strom Thurmond, a conservative from North Carolina, thus sewing up most of the delegates from the South. In exchange, Nixon promised that his running mate would not be a liberal Republican from the Northeast. At that even Ike caved in, with an endorsement on July 16, three weeks before the nominating convention.

On August 8, 1968, Richard M. Nixon received his second Republican nomination for president of the United States. In his acceptance speech he declared, "After an era of confrontation, the time has come for an era of negotiations with the leaders of Communist China and the Soviet Union"—hardly the words of a tough anti-Communist. He spoke also of children trapped in "a living nightmare of poverty, neglect and despair," who must be helped by government—scarcely the words of a conservative opposing government spending programs. Then Nixon also spoke, for the first time, about himself: "I see another child tonight. He hears a train go by at night and he dreams of faraway places where he'd like to go. It seems like an impossible dream. And tonight he stands before you, nominated for President of the United States of America. You can see why I believe so deeply in the American dream," he concluded. He ended by asking the delegates "to help me make the dream come true for millions to whom it's an impossible dream today."

To fill the bottom half of the ticket, Nixon chose Spiro

Agnew, the governor of Maryland, a comparative unknown who appealed to Nixon for several reasons. For one thing, he came from a border state, which would appeal to the South without alienating the North. He was also physically attractive, tall and broad shouldered. And he was a Greek-American, which might appeal to ethnic groups that usually voted Democratic. Furthermore, Agnew had gained a reputation for being a law-and-order governor: when riots had broken out in Baltimore in 1967, Agnew had summoned a group of prominent black civic leaders and berated them for not doing more to stop the disorders. This approach sat well with white Southerners.

Richard Nixon and his Vice-Presidential running mate, Maryland governor Spiro T. Agnew, wave to the delegates at the Republican national convention.

A HOUSE DIVIDED

In 1968 there were two key issues. The first was the Vietnam War, then in its fourth year with no end in sight. More than 40,000 American soldiers had been killed and 150,000 wounded. The financial cost exceeded $150 billion. It had squeezed out many ambitious domestic programs and driven up prices. Worse yet, the nation was in turmoil. There had been a rash of antiwar demonstrations, with many on college campuses.

The second issue was one either of civil rights (in the eyes of liberals) or law and order (as seen by conservatives). The legislative gains of the 1950s and 1960s, which had toppled many restrictions on voting and housing, had cured some ills in the South. But northern blacks, especially those in the larger cities, thought that more should be done about poverty and the strained relations between African-American communities and the police. In 1967, a presidential commission formed to investigate the disturbances concluded that America was fast becoming two societies—one white and rich, the other black and poor.

The United States had become, by 1968, a violent nation. In March, Martin Luther King, Jr., the leader of the nonviolent civil rights movement, was assassinated by a white supremacist. This event touched off rioting in many cities. To much of the public, antiwar demonstrations seemed nearly as frightening as riots, being the tense standoffs between students and police that they were.

The Democrats, who controlled the government, were dispirited and divided. President Johnson did win the New Hampshire Democratic primary, but just barely, edging out an antiwar opponent, Wisconsin senator Eugene McCarthy.

Johnson then announced that he was halting the bombing of North Vietnam, that he would seek peace talks with the North Vietnamese, and—most stunning of all—that he would not seek reelection. His vice-president, Hubert Humphrey, entered the race as a supporter of Johnson's war policy. Meanwhile, Eugene McCarthy and Robert F. Kennedy, a New York senator and brother of the slain president, dueled in a series of primaries for leadership of the antiwar element of the party. In June, Kennedy won the California primary, but he was then assassinated by a Palestinian named Sirhan Sirhan, who was protesting American support for Israel in its 1967 war with the Arabs.

The violence of 1968 was capped by the Democratic National Convention, held in Chicago. Inside the convention hall, Hubert Humphrey held a majority of the delegates and controlled the proceedings. On the streets outside, though, thousands of antiwar demonstrators clashed with police. Tear gas even wafted into the hotels where delegates and news reporters were staying. All this action was televised, live and in color, to 100 million American viewers. When it was over, the polls showed the Republicans ahead of the Democrats by 45 percent to 29 percent, with 18 percent of Americans favoring the third-party candidacy of George Wallace, the governor of Alabama.

THE 1968 ELECTION CAMPAIGN

Nixon was now in an ideal position. He proceeded to line up the factions of his party and secured promises of support both from liberals who had backed Rockefeller and conservatives who had favored Reagan. Avoiding now the fatal error of 1960, Nixon lavished time and money on the seven biggest states—California, Illinois, Michigan, New York, Ohio,

Pennsylvania, and Texas—with their combined electoral vote total of 210 (of the 270 needed for victory). This time he did not promise to campaign in all fifty states.

Yet Nixon's lead slowly shrank. One problem was that Spiro Agnew turned out to be a major liability. His assignment was to take the low road, as Nixon himself had done in 1952 and 1956. For Agnew, however, the low road ran through the gutter. For example, he made crude remarks about ethnic groups that offended many voters. Nixon ended up keeping his running mate at a distance. In fact, he never appeared with him and rarely even mentioned him. Still, as Democrats kept on reminding the public, Agnew was only "a heartbeat away" from the White House. Another problem was that Hubert Humphrey had recovered from the disaster of the Democratic convention. He now seized the initiative and challenged Nixon to debate on the issues. This was the last thing Nixon wanted, being still haunted by memories of Lazy-Shave. He thus refused to meet with his challenger, and soon Humphrey was referring to him as Richard the Silent and Richard the Chicken-Hearted.

The real crux of the 1968 campaign, however, was the war in Vietnam. The public wanted it to end, and expected Nixon to suggest a solution. He had long since abandoned his calls for "escalation"—more troops and heavier bombing. President Johnson had adopted these proposals, but they had fizzled. The enemy was able to hold its own in battle and the South Vietnamese still seemed unable to fend for themselves. Nixon's strategy was to announce a "moratorium" on discussing the war, to say nothing at all. He explained that he wanted to avoid jeopardizing delicate negotiations President Johnson was holding with the enemy. Nixon hinted that he had a "secret solution" to the war. Just as Eisenhower had extricated the United States from Korea in 1953, Nixon said, he would end the Vietnam War "with honor" in 1969.

In the final weeks of the campaign, Vietnam became the most important piece in the election game. President Johnson contacted the North Vietnamese government in Hanoi and offered to halt the bombing in return for holding peace talks. Nixon in turn warned the South Vietnamese of Johnson's plan. Their government then rejected the negotiations. Johnson announced them anyway, and Humphrey surged ahead in the polls. After the peace talks were denounced by South Vietnam, Nixon issued a statement saying that "the prospects for peace are not as bright as we would have hoped a few days ago." As election day neared, Nixon and Humphrey were in a dead heat.

THE ELECTION RESULTS

The 1968 election seemed, at first, like a replay of 1960. By 9:00 P.M. Nixon had an early lead. At ten o'clock the race was even. By eleven o'clock Humphrey was in front and seemed to be pulling away with the popular vote. Nixon stayed up all night. It was dawn before his aides could persuade him to close his eyes for a brief nap. At 8:30 A.M., one of his staff, Dwight Chapin, charged into his room. "ABC just declared you the winner!" he yelled. "You got it. You've won." Nixon went over to his wife, who burst into tears of joy.

In the final analysis, much of the South had gone for Nixon, as had the mountain states and most of the Middle West. Nixon lost New York, Michigan, Pennsylvania, Texas, and much of the Northeast, but he carried California, Illinois, and Ohio—enough of the "big seven" to give him 301 electoral college votes to Humphrey's 191 and Wallace's 46. The popular vote was much closer, though. Nixon got

31,770,237 votes (43.4 percent) to Humphrey's 31,270,533 (42.7 percent). Wallace's 9,906,141 votes gave him 13.5 percent, which was high for a third-party candidate.

Nixon went to the ballroom of the Waldorf-Astoria Hotel in New York to thank his supporters and campaign workers, most of whom had also stayed up all night. He wore a big smile and held up the first two fingers of both hands, his own "V for victory" sign. "Having lost a close one eight years ago and having won a close one this year," said the new president-elect, "I can say this—winning's a lot more fun." Then he told the crowd about something he had seen during the campaign, at a stop in Deshler, Ohio. There a teenager had held up a sign that said Bring Us Together. "That will be the great objective of this administration at the outset," said Richard M. Nixon: "to bring the American people together."

7

WAR AND PEACE

As Richard Nixon rode up Pennsylvania Avenue on January 20, 1969, for his inauguration, hundreds of antiwar demonstrators protested. At 13th Street his limousine was pelted with stones, beer cans, and bottles. It was the first major disruption of an inaugural ceremony in recent American history. "I shall consecrate my office, my energies, and all the wisdom I can summon to the cause of peace among nations," Nixon declared to the nation. This would mean ending the war in Vietnam, which was claiming the lives of about three hundred American soldiers each week.

THE "SECRET STRATEGY"
During the 1968 campaign Nixon had hinted that he had a secret strategy for ending the war. It soon became clear that this strategy was diplomatic. He hoped the Soviets and Chinese could be pressured to lead North Vietnam toward peace.

In July, Nixon announced a new policy. The United States would now begin to "Vietnamize" the war, as he characterized it. American ground troops would be gradually withdrawn, and the brunt of combat would then fall on the South

Vietnamese forces. Nixon changed the orders to his commanding general in Vietnam from "defeat the enemy" to "provide maximum assistance" to South Vietnam's military forces. But whenever the North Vietnamese launched new offensives, Nixon retaliated forcefully. He continued to bomb areas in South Vietnam controlled by the Communists and began bombing Cambodia, but secretly, in order to avoid new antiwar protests. "I will not be the first President of the United States," said Nixon, "to lose a war."

The antiwar protests continued. In December, Nixon announced the removal of another 50,000 troops. On April 20 he said that 150,000 troops would come home within the next twelve months, leaving 275,000 to carry on the war. This was only half the number that President Johnson had maintained, but opponents of the war were not yet satisfied with these troop cuts. By fall 1972 there were fewer than 20,000 American military support personnel left in Vietnam, roughly the number first sent over by President Kennedy in 1963. In three years Nixon had in fact successfully Vietnamized the ground combat.

NEGOTIATING PEACE

By late summer 1972 Hanoi was ready to talk about peace. On October 11 Nixon offered to call off the bombing of Hanoi and elsewhere. However, South Vietnam's president Nguyen van Thieu rejected these terms, which permitted the Communists to keep hundreds of thousands of troops in the South and included them in a coalition government. For Thieu the deal seemed an American surrender. Many conservative Republicans agreed, as did a number of top American military officers. On November 2, in a nationwide address just before the presidential election, Nixon announced new military aid to Vietnam.

Nixon's negotiator was his national security advisor, Henry Kissinger, formerly a professor of political science at Harvard University. Kissinger met in Paris with the North Vietnamese, who would not give an inch. Kissinger was frustrated. "They make the Russians look good," he said, "compared to the way the Russians make the Chinese look good when it comes to negotiating in a responsible and decent way." On December 14, 1972, just before Christmas, Nixon ordered new mining of Haiphong harbor and B-52 bomber strikes on industrial targets in Hanoi. Three B-52s were shot down on December 17 as the first raids were carried out. "We must continue until we get some sort of break," Nixon then wrote in his diary. After four more days of bombing, eight additional planes had been lost. Nixon offered to stop the air attacks if the North Vietnamese would agree to a meeting in early January. On December 29 he ordered a halt to them.

The bombings caused a furor in the United States. "The President has taken leave of his senses," Republican senator William Saxbe exclaimed. "War by tantrum" was the judgment of *New York Times* columnist James Reston. On January 2, 1973, Senate and House Democrats made plans to pass a law cutting off funding for military operations in Indochina. Congress would soon convene and vote to end the war. Nixon knew at this point that more bombing was no longer an option and the last military card had been played. Hanoi, too, was looking for a quick agreement. On January 9, 1973, the two sides agreed to a cease-fire, an exchange of prisoners, an accounting of those missing in action, and a complete American withdrawal. On January 15 all bombing of the North was halted.

On January 23, 1973, one day after former president Lyndon Johnson died, and three days after Richard Nixon was sworn in to his second term as president of the United

States, the Paris Peace Accords were completed and initialed by negotiators. Bombing continued in Cambodia, but was stopped by Congress on August 15, 1973. The American military involvement in Indochina was now over.

THE CHINA CARD

"We in the Nixon administration felt that our challenge was to educate the American people in the requirements of the balance of power," Kissinger wrote in his memoir, *Years of Upheaval.* The Nixon–Kissinger foreign policy was based on the concept of *realpolitik,* a German term that means dealing with the world as one finds it. Nixon's policies were formed on the basis of how nations actually seemed to behave and on a realistic assessment of American national interests.

Nixon wanted to use the power of the United States to reinforce alliances and dissuade adversaries from combining to defeat U.S. interests. His approach to the two Communist superpowers, the Soviet Union and the People's Republic of China, was to develop a policy of *détente,* a French word meaning a relaxation of tensions.

Nixon had long been a foe of Communist China. Soon after his inauguration, however, he began to work to improve relations with that nation, especially after its clash with the Soviet Union along their disputed border in 1969. This seemed a good time to drive a wedge between the two Communist powers. Nixon's first step was a small one, an exchange of sports teams between the United States and China. China sent over its table-tennis champions and "Ping-Pong Diplomacy" was born. In 1971, Kissinger indicated to Chinese premier Zhou En-lai that he wished to visit China and initiate talks. The Chinese were agreeable to this suggestion. Kissinger would be welcome in China to prepare for a summit conference between Nixon and Mao Zedong, the chairman of China's Communist party, the father of its revolution, and still, in his late seventies, the most powerful man in the land. Stephen Ambrose, one of Nixon's biographers, records Kissinger's elation upon receiving word of the accepted proposal: "This is the most important communication that has come to an American president since the end of World War II."

From November 1971 to 1973 Kissinger secretly met more than twenty times with Beijing's U.N. ambassador to discuss world issues, especially the Soviet threat to China. Nixon and Zhou made a deal. The United States for its part would withdraw all troops from Taiwan, an island which was ruled by a non-communist Chinese government (known as the Republic of China) that lay claim to all of China and held the Chinese seat in the United Nations. The United States would end its opposition to seating Communist China in the United Nations in place of the regime in Taiwan. The Chinese in turn would urge North Vietnam to reduce the level of combat in South Vietnam. On July 15, 1971, Nixon notified the American public that he personally would be visiting China. On October 25, 1971, the People's Republic of China was admitted to the United Nations and the Taiwan regime was expelled from the United Nations Security Council and General Assembly, with no American opposition.

NIXON VISITS CHINA

On February 17, 1972, thousands of Americans, including top government officials, gathered at Andrews Air Force Base near Washington to give Richard and Pat Nixon an enthusiastic send-off for their trip to China. "We can have differences without being enemies in war," Nixon said of the occasion.

"If we can make progress toward that goal on this trip, the world will be a much safer world." The Nixons' landing in Beijing was televised in the United States. Live coverage showed Nixon coming alone down the gangway of Air Force One. At the bottom of the gangway, the president was greeted by Zhou En-lai. As the two shook hands, many who were watching remembered how, in 1954, Secretary of State John Foster Dulles had refused to shake Zhou's hand at a diplomatic conference in Geneva. Nixon's handshake with Zhou now marked the beginning of a new era.

On the first day of his visit, Nixon was taken by Zhou to see Mao Zedong. The two men discussed world events for more than an hour. "The chairman's writings moved a nation and have changed the world," Nixon said of Mao, who beamed. Nixon flattered Mao again by noting that Mao had taken a risk in inviting him, but "I know that you are one who sees when an opportunity comes, and then knows that you must seize the hour and seize the day." This was a quotation from the *Writings of Mao Zedong*. Finally, Nixon told Mao, "Since you do not know me, you shouldn't trust me." But, he continued, "You will find that I never say something I cannot do. And I always will do more than I can say." For his part, Mao remarked that "your book, *Six Crises,* is not a bad book."

This conference was followed by a week of banquets and tours of Chinese historical sites, all of which was broadcast back to the United States. In particular, Nixon was awed by the Great Wall of China. "This is a great wall," he reportedly said, "and it had to be built by a great people."

In February 1972, Nixon and Zhou huddled for twenty hours in Shanghai, then issued what became known as the Shanghai communiqué. In it the two leaders agreed on one

President Nixon and his Chinese hosts tour the Great Wall of China. "It is a great wall, and it had to have been built by a great people," Nixon remarked.

crucial point: they would combat "hegemony"—meaning Soviet influence—in Asia. "We have set up a process where common ground can gradually be expanded," Nixon told his cabinet upon his return. "We have renounced the threat of force and the use of force against each other, as well as other nations; we agree that neither nation should dominate Asia."

Playing the China card turned out to be good politics as well as good diplomacy. In 1971, Nixon's approval rating with the American public had dipped below 50 percent in the polls, and it seemed possible that he might not win reelection. His success with China lifted his ratings to 55 percent, they soared past 60 percent during the election campaign.

THE MOSCOW SUMMIT

On May 22, 1972, Air Force One landed in Moscow, and Richard Nixon became the first U.S. president to set foot in the capital of the Soviet Union. The Nixons were installed in a suite in the Grand Palace of the Kremlin. The rest of the delegation stayed in a hotel overlooking Red Square, which was decked out with a large American flag. The most important document to be signed during this visit was the Basic Principles of Relations. It recognized that the Soviets had achieved parity with the United States as a superpower and that détente was the only desirable road to peace.

"I have a reputation of being a hard-line anti-Communist," Nixon admitted at an early meeting. "We know, we know," said Premier Alexei Kosygin. Soon the Soviet and American leaders locked horns. On May 24, at Leonid Brezhnev's *dacha*, or country home, the two leaders argued about the Vietnam War, then attended a small dinner where the atmosphere relaxed.

The following morning, at 2:00 A.M., while Nixon was getting a back massage, Kissinger reported that his own negotiators and the Joint Chiefs of Staff (the highest-ranking American military officers) opposed the agreement that Kissinger had been negotiating. Worse yet, the Soviets had failed to make the concessions Nixon had expected. "Go to your negotiations, Henry," Nixon replied. "Do the best you can. But we don't have to settle this week." Kissinger proceeded to warn the Soviets that Nixon was prepared to leave without signing an agreement. After the Russians conceded some points, an agreement was then signed.

These Nixon–Kissinger negotiations with the Soviets achieved a symbolic breakthrough in arms control and helped relax international tensions between the two superpowers. But the agreement did not reduce the quantity or quality of nuclear weapons. Hundreds of billions of dollars would continue to be spent on these weapons in the years to come. In fact, the number of warheads each side possessed more than doubled after the agreements were signed. When President Nixon returned to the United States from Moscow on June 1, 1972, he addressed a joint session of Congress. "We took the first step," he told them, "toward a new era of mutually agreed restraint and arms limitation."

Nixon concluded no further arms negotiations during his time in office, although Leonid Brezhnev came to Washington, D.C., for a second summit, on June 23, 1973. He and Nixon then conversed at length about China. Kissinger later recounted in his memoir that his counterpart, Soviet Foreign Secretary Andrei Gromyko, advised that "any military agreement between China and the United States would lead to war." The American president reassured the Soviet leader that the improving relations between the United States and China were not directed at harming the Soviets.

In the summer of 1974, Nixon and Kissinger attended their final summit in the Soviet Union. "Because of our personal relationship," Nixon said of himself and Brezhnev, "there is no question about our will to keep these agreements and to make more where they are in our mutual interests." The two leaders then reached some limited agreements.

In the light of subsequent events—specifically the collapse, in 1989-90, of Soviet control in Eastern Europe—Nixon's and Kissinger's ideas seemed prophetic, as a memo Kissinger sent Nixon in 1973 demonstrates. Just before the second summit meeting with Brezhnev in Washington, Kissinger noted that détente between the United States and the Soviet Union might ultimately transform the entire Soviet system. "Brezhnev's gamble is that as these policies gather momentum and longevity, their effects will not undermine the very system from which Brezhnev draws his power and legitimacy," Kissinger pointed out. "Our goal on the other hand is to achieve precisely such effects over the long run." Nixon and Kissinger realized that if the cold war's tensions decreased and the Soviets could be drawn into cooperative economic and scientific relationships, their very system of Communist rule might be subject to Westernizing influence. As Kissinger later put it in his memoirs: "If the West saw to containment, I was convinced that it would win its historical bet. The Soviet Union's economic system was glaringly weak; its ideological appeal had faded, its political base and empire were precarious."

Nixon and Kissinger fashioned détente to contain Soviet power and draw Soviet and Chinese leaders into closer relations with the West. In large measure, they succeeded. If they did not effectively limit the arms race, at least they did put limits on Soviet–American tensions. That in turn paved the way for the eventual thawing of the cold war.

8

Domestic Policy

Like many other presidents, Richard Nixon was often bored by domestic affairs. "You really only need a president for foreign affairs," he suggested to John Kennedy after the 1960 elections. "For domestic affairs the cabinet could run the country." Nixon knew, however, that voters often pay less attention to global issues than to matters that were closer to home. His own constituency expected him to reduce the size of the federal government, cut back on spending and taxes, and minimize congressional participation in affairs that could be managed as well if not better by state and local governments.

CIVIL RIGHTS

For most of his political life, Richard Nixon had supported civil rights legislation. For instance, as vice-president he had chaired a committee to end racial discrimination among employers who received federal contracts. And when he had presided over the Senate, he had ruled in favor of senators trying to pass legislation to protect minorities. Later, Nixon had supported the Civil Rights Act of 1964, which guaranteed minorities equal access to public facilities, and the Voting

Rights Act of 1965, which provided federal protection to blacks voting in southern states.

By the late 1960s, however, new civil rights issues were arising that were not as clear-cut, both to Nixon and to many others. Should students be bused out of their own neighborhoods to establish a racially balanced mix in the public schools? Should the government enforce hiring laws that favored minority ethnic groups and women when opponents were arguing that these laws were themselves discriminatory and would only worsen the problem they were meant to solve?

There was also the question of politics. In 1968, Nixon had captured only 12 percent of the African-American vote, and he was not likely to do any better in 1972. His support from this group was low because he had courted southern whites,

President Nixon meets with civil rights leaders in the cabinet room of the White House to discuss his plans for additional government funding for inner-city schools.

many of whom had objected to the existing civil rights programs. In his first inaugural address Nixon indicated that there would be no new civil rights initiatives in his administration. "The laws have caught up with our consciences," he said, although he did pledge to "give life to what is in the law." At the same time, his attorney general, John Mitchell, told African-American leaders that they should "watch what we do, not what we say." By this he meant that Nixon might "talk tough" but would still act to advance the cause of minorities.

In the 1960s, southern school districts began to desegregate, in compliance with federal law. Districts that were found to have been dragging their feet were denied funds by the Johnson administration. Even so, when Nixon took office 82 percent of the black children in the South were attending public schools that were at least 95 percent black. Here was a sensitive issue. According to a 1969 Gallup poll, 44 percent of the American people thought that integration was moving too fast, 22 percent thought it was not going fast enough, and 25 percent thought the pace about right.

Nixon cast his lot with the 44 percent plurality. On July 3, 1969, the Department of Health, Education and Welfare (HEW) extended the deadlines for desegregation in some districts and ended the practice of cutting off federal funds to districts that refused to desegregate. "It's almost enough to make you vomit," said Roy Wilkins, a prominent black leader. "This is not a matter of too little too late; rather, this is nothing at all." In 1970, Nixon ordered George Shultz, his secretary of labor, to set up advisory committees formed of black and white civil leaders in many southern school districts. These committees then helped break down local resistance to integration.

The "two societies" that Robert Coles described of this period existed not only in the South. Half the black schoolchildren in the North and the West also attended predominantly black schools, where segregation arose from housing patterns rather than out of state law. Courts had ordered that pupils be bused into schools outside their neighborhoods, to balance enrollment. Nixon called busing "a new evil... disrupting communities and imposing hardship on children—both black and white." The matter was up to the courts, though, not the president. Some judges ordered black children to attend schools that were predominantly white, and vice versa. Nixon objected, as did many citizens. A November 1971 Gallup poll indicated that 76 percent of the public, including 47 percent of all blacks, were opposed to busing.

In March 1972, Nixon asked Congress to impose a "moratorium" on the power of the federal courts to order busing to enforce desegregation. He also called for $2.5 billion in new federal aid to upgrade inner-city schools, "so that the children who go there will have just as good a chance to get quality education as do children who go to school in the suburbs." The Democratic-controlled Congress, which favored busing, refused to pass the legislation. Nixon's approach was upheld by the Supreme Court in 1974 when it ruled that busing could not be required in suburban school districts having no history of racial discrimination.

JOBS AND PROGRESS

Nixon, himself a tireless worker, believed that jobs held the key to social advancement. For this reason he directed George Shultz to devise a plan to increase the number of black construction workers. This plan specifically targeted Philadelphia, where the federal government had $4 billion in construction contracts. Federal contractors there were directed to submit "letters of commitment." Each such letter amounted to a promise that, within the space of four years, the percentage of blacks hired by the contractor would climb from 4 percent to at least 26 percent. This Philadelphia Plan, as it came to be called, was eventually adopted in New York, Pittsburgh, Seattle, Los Angeles, St. Louis, San Francisco, Boston, Chicago, and Detroit.

The Nixon administration also provided federal loans and grants to businesses owned and operated by minorities. When Nixon had entered office in 1969, only $8 million in government contracts then went to blacks and Hispanics. By 1972 this figure had jumped to $242 million. Grants and loans had increased similarly, from $200 million to $472 million.

REVERSING GENDER DISCRIMINATION

The Equal Pay Act of 1963 had required federal contractors to pay women workers the same wages they paid men. In 1971 this law was extended by Congress to cover the executive, administrative, and professional employees of all organizations receiving federal funds. The Nixon administration agreed with this. It required that every company with fifty employees or more that did more than $50,000 annually in federal business must move women into jobs from which they had traditionally been excluded. A year later, Congress passed Title IX of the Education Amendments of 1972. It prohibited discrimination on the basis of sex by any educational program or activity receiving federal financial assistance. This law was interpreted by the Nixon administration to mean that all activities—not just those earmarked for federal funds—must be free of discrimination. The result was a vast increase in the number of women enrolling in colleges and professional schools, as well as a dramatic expansion of women's athletic programs in high schools and colleges.

WELFARE REFORM

Nothing irked conservatives more than the federal welfare system. By 1969, it was costing $4 billion annually to provide small cash grants to 15 million poor people (two-thirds white, one-third minorities). Roughly one child in ten was then on the welfare rolls. Welfare regulations declared families with a husband or "man in the house" present to be ineligible for assistance. And when someone obtained a job, the benefits were completely cut off. These regulations gave welfare recipients little incentive either to create a stable family or to obtain a job.

"This whole thing smells to high heaven and we should get charging on it immediately," Nixon told Daniel Patrick Moynihan, a former Harvard University professor whom Nixon had named secretary of his Urban Affairs Council. Moynihan came up with a proposal for family allowances, meaning cash payments made directly to families that were intact. This system set a uniform standard payment throughout the entire nation and actually increased the number of eligible recipients. In fact, it was discovered that the program would cost an additional $4.4 billion. Nixon was nevertheless willing to spend this additional money on programs, if they provided training and jobs. The Moynihan plan even proposed having day-care services so that children could be taken care of while their parents worked. Nixon and Moynihan wanted a plan that would make people who accepted training better off than those who snubbed it, and people who got jobs better off than the unemployed. The income and Social Security taxes paid by new workers might be expected to meet some of the costs of the new program. The existing welfare system, Nixon told his cabinet, was "a social disaster and I'm not going to take one more step down that road."

In an address to the nation on August 8, 1969 Nixon described the shortcomings of the established welfare system. "It breaks up homes. It often penalizes work. It robs recipients of dignity. And it grows." Nixon's proposal was greeted with skepticism, however. A Gallup poll showed that 57 percent of the public opposed having a guaranteed income. The House approved the plan, but the Senate rejected it.

Nixon had better luck reforming other parts of the welfare system. For example, he tripled assistance to the blind, the disabled, and the elderly and changed the rules so that twice the number of people qualified for these funds.

NEW STRATEGIES IN THE WAR ON POVERTY

Nixon rejected the Democratic approach to poverty, saying there was too much red tape and waste in it. "Our job," he said, "is to get resources to people in need and then to let them run their own lives." To the extent that social services might be needed, they should, in Nixon's view, be paid for and provided by state and local governments. He tried to dismantle programs initiated by the Democrats, but he was often checked by Congress and the courts.

Nixon's war on poverty programs was not completely thwarted, however. He managed to slice the $2 billion budget of the Office of Economic Opportunity (OEO) in half. Nixon was willing to spend money directly on the poor, but he distrusted the OEO and its legion of social workers, antipoverty workers, poverty lawyers, and others who worked with the poor to provide them with services. He thought these professionals were wasting government resources.

A case in point is Nixon's approach to hunger. In the 1960s, Americans who suffered from hunger or malnutrition qualified to receive food distributed by county welfare officials. This plan flopped, because often the food was low in nutritional value. In 1968, Congress created a Select Committee on Nutrition and Human Needs. This body reported back that there was widespread malnutrition among the poor. Then, in 1969, the Nixon administration sponsored a White House Conference on Food, Nutrition, and Health. "The moment is at hand to put an end to hunger in America itself," the president declared. Nixon's staff worked closely with Senate Republicans and devised a new plan that provided stamps that the poor could use to buy food in supermarkets. The administration provided $1.1 billion for this program in 1969, and by the end of Nixon's first term the program was making available $8 billion worth of food to the poor.

BACK TO THE SOURCE

"For years now, the trend has been to sweep more and more authority toward Washington," Nixon told voters during his 1968 presidential campaign. "Too many decisions that would have been better been made in Seattle or St. Louis have wound up on the president's desk." When Nixon assumed office, the total cost of federal programs was more than $20 billion a year. He proposed that programs involving local matters, such as education and law enforcement, be turned over to the state and local governments. Nixon's argument was that these governments would be more responsive and efficient and more accountable to the people they served than would the national government.

In his state of the Union address on January 22, 1971, Nixon called for a $16 billion investment in "renewing state and local government." He wanted $5 billion in unrestricted "revenue sharing" each year to go to states and localities. Another $11 billion would be shifted away from thirty-one narrow categories of federal programs (such as to build hospitals or roads or provide vocational training) and given instead to states for such broad purposes as health, community development, employment and job training, and law enforcement. This proposal, which was designated the New Federalism, would allow state and local officials new flexibility in using national funds. After a tussle in Congress the bill passed, and on October 20, 1972, Nixon signed the State and Local Fiscal Assistance Act at Independence Hall in Philadelphia. He said the program would "renew the American federal system created in Philadelphia two centuries earlier."

The New Federalism program did not last long. A later Republican president, Ronald Reagan, persuaded Congress to eliminate it. Nixon, it turned out, had in fact upped federal spending. During the Nixon years alone, the cost of domestic programs jumped from $20 billion to $35 billion—hardly a reduction of power for Washington. Richard Nixon's last budget, submitted in January 1974, actually provided 58 percent more funding for domestic social programs than had the last budget submitted by Lyndon Johnson, his "big spending" Democratic predecessor.

9

CRIMES AND MISDEMEANORS

Shortly before 2:00 A.M. on June 17, 1972, Frank Wills, a security guard, made the rounds of the Watergate, a luxury apartment and office complex in Washington, D.C. He noticed that the garage door had been tampered with and called the police. Three minutes later, a squadron appeared and inspected the building; they could tell that something had happened on the sixth floor. The officers entered a suite of offices, switched on the lights, and shouted, "Come out! Police!" A man replied, "Be careful, you got us." There were with him four others, who had all broken into the suite nearly an hour before.

The next day, the local newspapers reported the incident as being merely a routine break-in. But there was a curious twist to it. This particular Watergate suite belonged to the Democratic National Committee, and this was a presidential election year. Slowly, the truth leaked out. To begin with, the burglars were linked to E. Howard Hunt, Jr., a low-level official in Richard Nixon's Committee to Re-Elect the President (CREEP). Hunt was then traced to a larger operation that involved important officials in the Nixon administration.

Someone—either a White House staffer or Nixon's campaign chairman, John N. Mitchell—had authorized the break-in.

PLUMBERS AT WORK

There is no direct evidence that Richard Nixon himself knew about the Watergate burglary, but the operation was of a piece with other activities in the Nixon White House. The president had illegally wiretapped and bugged newspaper reporters and officials in his own administration. And he had used the FBI illegally, to spy on antiwar organizations. Within the White House itself, a group of men known as the plumbers had plotted secret break-ins of offices belonging to Nixon's "enemies," as the president called his opponents. Some of the plumbers had joined CREEP. Then Mitchell, its chief, approved Operation Gemstone, a plan to pry into the dealings of Lawrence O'Brien, the chairman of the Democratic National Committee, and various others who might have had damaging information on Nixon's personal finances.

As soon as he heard the first news reports, the president telephoned his chief of staff, H. R. Haldeman. "What does it matter?" Nixon asked. "The American people will see it for what it was: a political prank. Hell, they can't take a break-in at the D.N.C. *seriously.* There's nothing there." White House press secretary Ronald L. Ziegler characterized it as "a third-rate burglary."

Perhaps; but it involved important people. It soon came out that the five men arrested at the Watergate had been there to repair a "bug" they had placed on O'Brien's phone in an earlier visit. These five were placed under custody along with their leader, James W. McCord, Jr., the head of security for CREEP. The White House feared that McCord, if pressed by police, might name his own supervisor, G. Gordon Liddy, the

CRIMES AND MISDEMEANORS

general counsel to CREEP, as an accomplice. Liddy in turn could then be linked to E. Howard Hunt and Hunt to White House aide Charles Colson. It might come out eventually that CREEP had given Liddy $200,000 in cash to fund his illegal operations. The "third-rate" break-in could then have been linked to the White House and to Mitchell, a former attorney general of the United States.

The story refused to go away as Nixon had hoped it would. On June 20, Nixon met with H. R. Haldeman and another aide, John D. Erlichman, to discuss their options. Two days later, Nixon stated that "the White House has had no involvement whatever in this particular incident." The next day, Nixon met again with his two top aides. They suggested now that the Central Intelligence Agency (CIA) be told that

President Nixon meets with his top advisors in the Oval Office. At left is H. R. "Bob" Haldeman, his chief of staff. At right is John Erlichman, White House counsel and advisor on domestic issues.

the break-in had involved a top-secret matter of national security and that an FBI investigation must be impeded. "Don't go any further into this case, period!" Nixon wanted Haldeman to tell the FBI. Another obstacle was the Justice Department, which was also asking questions. White House aides meanwhile shredded files and burned evidence about Operation Gemstone. Nixon himself approved a plan to offer "hush money" to the burglars to keep them from revealing their link to the White House.

Nixon told the nation that no one "presently employed" by the White House had been involved in this "bizarre incident." The Democratic National Committee filed suit against CREEP, but trial was postponed until after the election. Nixon acted to quiet the scandal. John Mitchell resigned. Some White House aides were sent away. Altogether these measures paid off. Public attention turned away from the "caper," as *Newsweek* called it, and toward the national conventions of the two major parties. In August 1972, Nixon was renominated, to face Democrat George McGovern, a senator from South Dakota and a strong liberal.

With a strong economy and good prospects for a cease-fire in Vietnam, Nixon was reelected by a landslide. He received 60.7 percent of the votes, the third-best showing in American history, to McGovern's 38 percent. However, the Republicans gained only twelve seats in the House and even lost two in the Senate. A Democratic Congress would be handling the Watergate investigation as Nixon began his second term.

THE TRUTH LEAKS OUT

The Watergate burglars were tried in a federal district court and convicted of breaking and entering. Judge John Sirica, a tough "law and order" judge, thought that receiving long sentences might induce the men to reveal who was behind the Watergate operation. Meanwhile, continuing prosecutions were leading directly to the White House, and the Senate was about to launch an investigation of its own. Nixon and his aides agreed that if the probe went too far they would blame John Mitchell. Another possible "fall guy" was John W. Dean III, the White House counsel. However, Dean went to the Justice Department on his own and made a confession. His accusations reached to the Oval Office.

On April 30, 1973, Haldeman and Erlichman resigned, as did Mitchell's replacement as attorney general, Richard Kleindienst. Watergate had now become a crisis. Nixon spoke to the nation that evening to deny any personal knowledge of the break-in or the cover-up. *The New York Times* reported that during this speech the president's voice quavered and his hands shook as he promised that "justice will be pursued, fairly, fully and impartially, no matter who is involved."

In the spring of 1973, the Senate Select Committee on Presidential Activities, chaired by North Carolina Democrat Sam Ervin, began televised hearings. The star witness was John Dean. He implicated Nixon in the cover-up, but there was no evidence to back up his story. Then one of Haldeman's aides, Alexander Butterfield, testified that the White House routinely taped conversations held in the Oval Office. The Senators realized that these might contain vital evidence. Nixon agreed to provide only summaries of some of the tapes, insisting that he had the right under "executive privilege" to keep other material confidential that was essential to his job as president. A federal court backed him up in this.

Meanwhile, the Ervin committee discovered that Nixon's reelection campaign had violated major campaign laws. Some involved funding. Candidates are not allowed to accept money from corporations, which can be capable of raising vast war chests and thus buying political favors. CREEP had failed to obey this law. In 1972 it had invited businesses to funnel large sums—as much as $250,000—into Nixon's reelection campaign. The Senate committee also learned that John Dean had used the Internal Revenue Service (IRS) to harass people on Nixon's "enemies list." Also, the administration had put illegal wiretaps on numerous officials. The psychiatrist of antiwar activist Daniel Ellsberg had been the target of a break-in by White House "plumbers" seeking damaging information on Ellsberg. It even turned out that Nixon had evaded paying some personal taxes. He owed $432,787 to the IRS and $75,000 to the state of California.

In August 1973, polls showed that 60 percent of the public wanted Nixon to remain in office, 20 percent favored his resignation, and 10 percent called for Congress to begin impeachment proceedings. Most of the public believed Nixon when he told them, at a press conference, "Your president is not a crook."

"NOLO CONTENDERE"

The same could not be said, however, for Nixon's vice-president. Since 1962, Spiro Agnew had been receiving cash payments from a Baltimore engineer and developer named Lester Matz, who in turn was given contracts to build government facilities. Agnew had been the executive of Baltimore County when he had first accepted the bribes. Then they continued while he was governor of Maryland and on into 1971, when he was vice-president. On October 9, 1973, the vice-president pleaded *nolo contendere*—a legal term that means, in Latin, "no contest"—to a lesser charge, income tax evasion. Agnew was spared a jail sentence but resigned his office.

Nixon now had to nominate a new vice-president. He consulted with congressional leaders and several hundred Republican party officials before finally choosing House minority leader Gerald R. Ford. The members of Congress were relieved. Should it become necessary to remove Richard Nixon from office, an acceptable vice-president would be available to assume the top office.

Agnew's resignation left a permanent scar on the Nixon administration. Support for Nixon's removal or resignation soared to more than 50 percent by January 1974. Public opinion could change, but evidence was another matter: if the Senate turned up enough damaging facts, Nixon knew he would face removal. His only hope was to control the investigation. But Nixon's new attorney general, Elliot L. Richardson, worked out a contrary arrangement with the Senate. Richardson would appoint a special prosecutor who would be free to pursue his own investigation. For this Richardson chose Archibald Cox, a distinguished professor at Harvard Law School. Richardson made a deal with the Senate that Cox could be removed from office only if he were ever to be proved guilty of "extraordinary improprieties"—that is, if Cox himself broke the law.

For Nixon this plan was a disaster. When Cox learned about the White House tapes, he demanded that Nixon turn them over. Judge Sirica agreed, but Nixon refused to comply. The conflict went to a higher court, which backed Sirica. Nixon now surrendered some of the tapes, but he instructed Cox not to press for more. Cox then won a court order requiring Nixon to turn over nine contested tapes. Nixon offered to provide summaries but not the actual tapes themselves. Cox spurned this compromise, which made Nixon furious. On October 20, 1973, he ordered Elliot Richardson to fire Cox. Instead, Richardson resigned in protest. The order to fire Cox then fell to Deputy Attorney General William D. Ruckelshaus. When he refused, he too was fired.

At last Nixon found an official who would obey his orders, Robert H. Bork, the solicitor general. His regular responsibility was to argue government cases before the Supreme Court. Bork agreed to fire Cox. FBI agents arrived at the offices of Cox, Richardson, and Ruckelshaus and prevented them from

Demonstrators near the White House demanded that President Nixon resign or be impeached after he fired special prosecutor Archibald Cox. Cox had sought to obtain White House tapes that would indicate the extent of Nixon's involvement in the Watergate scandal.

removing any files, or even their personal belongings. This episode, dubbed the Saturday Night Massacre, loosed a storm of protest. Nixon buckled, and promised he would release the nine tapes that Cox had demanded. These tapes in due course reached the grand jury that was hearing the case. But by then an eighteen-and-a-half-minute segment had been erased from one of them, material recorded during the first meeting Nixon had held with Erlichman and Haldeman after the Watergate break-in. Nixon denied knowing anything about the missing segment or who might have erased it. By this time public trust in him was fading.

IMPEACHMENT

Within a few days of the Saturday Night Massacre, twenty-two bills had been introduced in the House calling for impeachment proceedings to begin. The House Judiciary Committee began to hold hearings. The key question involved interpretation: what, exactly, constituted a "high crime and misdemeanor," this being the only ground on which a president might be removed from office? Most Republicans on the Judiciary Committee agreed with Nixon, who contended in a press conference that "a criminal offense on the part of the President is the requirement for impeachment." Democrats generally argued that "the Framers [of the Constitution] intended impeachment to be a constitutional safeguard of the public trust." If the president were to exceed the powers of his office or "behave in a manner grossly incompatible with the proper function and purpose of the office," he could be impeached.

The House committee deliberated until July 27, 1974. On that day, six Republicans out of seventeen voted with all twenty-one Democrats for the first article of impeachment.

"Richard M. Nixon, using the powers of his high office," the first article stated, "engaged personally and through his subordinates and agents in a course of conduct or plan designed to delay, impede and obstruct investigations... to cover up, conceal, and protect those responsible and to conceal the existence and scope of other unlawful activities."

The second article of impeachment charged Nixon with using government agencies like the CIA, FBI, Secret Service, and IRS to harass opponents of the administration and obstruct the administration of justice. It also charged him with maintaining "a secret investigative unit within the office of the President" that "engaged in covert and unlawful activities."

The third article cited Nixon's refusal to answer committee subpoenas for evidence, which had impeded the impeachment inquiry. The committee concluded that by obstructing the inquiry the president had "acted in a manner contrary to his trust as President and subversive of constitutional government" and that this had caused "manifest injury to the people of the United States."

Both the second and the third articles were also approved by the Judiciary Committee.

THE SUPREME COURT DECIDES

Nixon's last hope was the Supreme Court. Would it permit him to withhold evidence from the special prosecutor? Nixon maintained that he alone could determine what evidence to turn over to the grand jury. The special prosecutor argued instead that in matters involving criminal offenses the special demands of the president must yield to the right of the grand jury to seek evidence. On July 24, 1974, in *United States* v. *Nixon*, the Supreme Court handed down its decision in a unanimous opinion written by Chief Justice Warren E. Burger. Nixon would have to turn over the tapes, along with other evidence, to the federal district court judge who was trying the Watergate cases.

Nixon complied with the decision of the Supreme Court and turned the tapes over to Leon Jaworski, the special prosecutor. One of them (made on June 23, 1972) indicated that Nixon had conspired to cover up White House involvement in Watergate by using the CIA, which was itself a crime and an impeachable offense. Republican Senate minority leader Hugh Scott, after reading the transcript, called it "a shabby, disgusting, immoral performance by all those involved." Newspaper publisher William Randolph Hearst, Jr., a member of the California publishing family that had backed Nixon throughout his entire career, called Nixon "a man totally immersed in the cheapest and sleaziest kind of conniving."

Even Nixon's supporters on the Judiciary Committee conceded that "the charges of conspiracy to obstruct justice, and obstruction of justice... may be taken as substantially confessed by Mr. Nixon." The committee concluded that the president had "committed certain acts for which he should have been impeached and removed from office."

DISGRACE

According to the contemporary polls, more than three-fifths of the public believed Nixon should not remain in office. On August 7 a delegation of senior Republicans met with President Nixon. At that time he admitted that he was thinking of resigning. "Mr. President," Senator Barry Goldwater replied, "if it comes to a trial in the Senate, I don't think you can count on more than fifteen votes." In fact, Goldwater told

Nixon waves to his White House staff for the last time before departing for Andrews Air Force Base, where a jet was waiting to fly him home to California. In a few hours the first resignation of an American president would go into effect.

CRIMES AND MISDEMEANORS

Nixon that even he was thinking of voting for impeachment. "I don't have many alternatives, do I?" the president asked bleakly. The senators did not respond. "Never mind," Nixon continued. "There'll be no tears from me."

After this meeting with the members of Congress, Nixon told his family that he would resign. The White House photographer Ollie Atkins was summoned for a last commemorative portrait. Julie burst into tears. "I love you, Daddy," she cried, as her father comforted her.

The following morning Nixon met with Vice President Ford. "Jerry, you'll do a good job," he said. For seventy minutes they discussed foreign policy issues. "From now on, Jerry, you are Mr. President," he told Ford as they parted, their eyes filled with tears. Shortly after noon Nixon's press secretary informed reporters that the president would make an address that evening on radio and television from the Oval Office. The family spent the day packing. That evening Nixon met briefly with congressional leaders and then with forty-six of his congressional supporters. "I just hope," he told them with moist eyes, "that you don't feel that I let you down."

At 9:00 P.M. on August 8, 1974, Nixon went on national television. "In the past few days," he told his last nationwide television audience, "it has become evident that I no longer have a strong enough political base in the Congress. . . . I have never been a quitter," he noted, but "as President I must put the interests of America first." Then came historic words: "I shall resign the Presidency effective at noon tomorrow."

10

THE NIXON PRESIDENCY

On August 22, 1974, the House Judiciary Committee released its 528-page final report, which the full House then approved, by a vote of 412 to 3. It said that "clear and convincing evidence" existed that Richard Nixon had obstructed justice and had "condoned, encouraged, and in some instances directed, coached, and personally helped to fabricate" perjury by his White House aides in covering up the Wategate crimes. It also stated that he had abused the powers of his office by misusing the CIA, the FBI, and the IRS. If he were to be tried and convicted for these crimes, Nixon would face more than thirty years' imprisonment.

THE COMEBACK TRAIL
After he resigned, Richard Nixon and his family returned to California to rebuild their lives in their new home, La Casa Pacifica. For a while things only got worse and worse. The Watergate special prosecutor continued legal actions against the ex-president. Nixon resigned from the California Supreme Court and the California bar, but the New York Bar Association instituted disbarment proceedings against him that prevented him from practicing law in New York. An array of

individual lawsuits nearly bankrupted the former president, who was to spend $1.8 million on legal fees over the next sixteen years.

On September 8, 1974, Richard Nixon received a presidential pardon from his successor, Gerald Ford. "No words can describe the depths of my regret and pain at the anguish my mistakes over Watergate have caused the nation and the presidency," Nixon said. A few days later he entered the hospital for treatment of a blood clot in his leg and had an operation. "Listen, Dick, we almost lost you last night," his doctor told him the next morning. Four transfusions were needed to save him from dying of postoperative shock. Nixon told his wife he did not think he was going to make it. "Don't talk that way," Pat said, gripping his hand. "You have got to make it. You must not give up." In the hospital he learned that his party had just suffered a massive defeat in the 1974 midterm congressional elections.

Nixon returned home to begin the long process of recovery. Swimming and golf helped; within a year he had regained his health. His presidential pension ($60,000) took care of his living expenses, and $300,000 from the federal government enabled him to pay the costs of leaving office. But there were still attorneys to pay. Nixon recovered his financial health by writing his memoirs for a hefty fee and by giving a television interview to David Frost, for the reported sum of $750,000. Nixon wrote six more books, most of them bestsellers, including several volumes that focused on foreign affairs. He was treated as a respected elder statesman on private visits to England, France, China, and twenty-three other countries. In the 1980s he was often consulted by President Reagan regarding world affairs, and in 1986 he was featured in a *Newsweek* cover story entitled "He's Back." He also appeared on the cover of *Time* and on network talk shows.

Nixon's friends raised $21 million to build the Richard Nixon Library and Birthplace, which opened in Yorba Linda, California, his boyhood hometown, in 1990. The Nixons themselves contributed $2 million of the total. Next to the library building is the simple white frame house where he was born. The library contains exhibits of the Nixon presidency but not Nixon's presidential papers. The former president successfully sued the government to keep 150,000 pages of those papers out of the hands of scholars.

Former presidents Ford and Reagan and President Bush all attended the dedication ceremony, along with some forty thousand onlookers. Future generations, Bush said, would remember Nixon "for dedicating his life to the greatest cause offered any president—the cause of peace among nations." Nixon spoke about perseverance in the face of adversity. "It is sad to lose," he told the crowd at the ceremony, "but the greatest sadness is to travel through life without knowing either victory or defeat."

In 1976 Pat Nixon suffered a stroke, but she regained much of her health through physical therapy. The Nixons then returned east and retired to a large, lovely house in Saddle River, New Jersey, an affluent suburb of New York City. An avid sports fan, Nixon attended the occasional baseball, football, and basketball game. He and Pat spent many hours with their children and grandchildren. And he walked four miles a day, like one of his heroes, French president Charles de Gaulle.

AFTER THE FALL

Richard Milhous Nixon was a man of great talent and vision who tried to use the presidency for great ends. He established new relationships with China and the Soviet Union and withdrew American forces from Vietnam. His ideas about decentralizing government programs, strengthening state governments, and providing the poor with greater work incentives were all adopted by subsequent presidents.

Nixon the statesman was tarnished by Nixon the politician. He campaigned as hard as any politician who had ever lived, but not always honorably. His missteps—some of them large ones—came back to haunt him. No president, it seems has taken less pleasure in his office. Nixon felt surrounded by treacherous foes and even went so far as to compile an "enemies list." He wiretapped everyone who came into the Oval Office, including his own top aides. He demanded written resignations from his entire cabinet at the beginning of his second term, just to show them who was boss. The White House under him was an unhappy place, and by the last year of the Nixon presidency it was a lonely place as well. Nixon had by then secluded himself, and few people other than his closest aides interrupted his brooding. In the last six weeks of Nixon's presidency he went off to retreats such as Camp David and spent only six days in the White House itself.

In *Breach of Faith*, Theodore White, a long-time observer of the presidency, wrote that Americans believe "that no matter how the faith may be betrayed elsewhere, at one particular point—the Presidency—justice will be done beyond prejudice, beyond rancor, beyond the possibility of a fix." Nixon betrayed this trust and shattered this myth, but justice was eventually done.

What was Nixon's legacy? He brought peace to a nation that had been at war for a decade and improved relations with our main adversaries, China and the Soviet Union. But he also soured the American people on politics and deepened their cynicism about government. He left a nation divided and demoralized, with its diplomatic affairs in disarray and its domestic agenda stalled. Jimmy Carter defeated Gerald Ford in 1976 by promising a government "as good as the people" and pledging "never to lie to you." However, it would take more than a new president to heal the breach of faith caused by Richard Nixon. "We the People of the United States of America"—all of us—would have to join in the effort to heal our politics and "create a more Perfect Union."

IMPORTANT DATES IN THE LIFE OF RICHARD M. NIXON

1913   Born on January 9 in Yorba Linda, California.
1925   Brother Arthur dies at age seven.
1926   Voted president and became valedictorian of his eighth-grade class.
1929   Defeated in election for president of student body at Whittier Union High School.
1930   Graduates from Whittier Union High School, third in his class.
1933   Brother Harold dies at age twenty-three. Elected student-body president of Whittier College.
1934   Graduates from Whittier College, second in his class.
1936   Elected president of Duke Law School student bar association.
1937   Graduates from Duke Law School, third in his class. Becomes a member of the California bar and begins practicing law in Whittier and La Habra.
1940   Marries Thelma Catherine "Pat" Ryan.

1942 Joins Office of Price Administration in Washington, D.C., as staff attorney.
1942–45 Serves in U.S. Navy in Pacific.
1946 Elected to House of Representatives from Whittier; defeats incumbent Jerry Voorhis; daughter Tricia born.
1948 Daughter Julie born.
1950 Defeats incumbent Helen Gahagan Douglas to become U.S. senator from California.
1952 Delivers "Checkers" speech.
Elected Vice President of the United States.
1956 Elected to second term as Vice President of the United States.
1958 Tours Latin America.
1960 Nominated by the Republican National Convention for President of the United States; defeated in general election by John F. Kennedy.
1962 Defeated by Governor Edmund "Pat" Brown in race for governor of California.
1963 Becomes partner in New York law firm Nixon, Mudge, Rose, Guthrie and Alexander.
1966 Begins political comeback by campaigning successfully for Republican candidates for the House of Representatives.
1968 Elected president of the United States, defeating Hubert Humphrey.
1969 Sworn in as the thirty-seventh president of the United States.
Announces policy of "Vietnamization" and gradual

IMPORTANT DATES

	withdrawal of American troops from South Vietnam.
1970	Orders the invasion of Cambodia.
1972	Becomes first U.S. president to visit China; meets with Soviet leader Leonid Brezhnev to inaugurate period of détente.
	Democratic National Committee headquarters in Watergate is burglarized by White House "plumbers" group; Nixon orders a cover-up of White House involvement in the crimes.
	Reelected president of the United States, defeating George McGovern.
1973	Agreement on Ending War and Restoring Peace (the Paris Peace Accords) is signed with North Vietnam in Paris.
	Fires key White House aides involved in Watergate scandal.
	Summit meeting at Camp David and San Clemente with Soviet leader Leonid Brezhnev.
	Vice President Spiro Agnew resigns as the result of a corruption scandal.
	Congress passes War Powers Act to regulate presidential warmaking.
	Fires Special Prosecutor Cox and Attorney General Elliot Richardson in the Saturday Night Massacre.
1974	Summit in Moscow with Leonid Brezhnev to sign accord on antiballistic missiles.
	Supreme Court rejects Nixon's claim of executive privilege and rules he must turn over White House

tapes to a federal court investigating Watergate crimes.

House Judiciary Committee votes to recommend impeachment of Nixon.

Resigns as president of the United States on August 9; succeeded by Vice President Gerald Ford.

1978 Publishes *RN: The Memoirs of Richard Nixon.*

FURTHER READING

BIOGRAPHIES

Ambrose, Stephen. *Nixon.* 2 vols. New York: Simon & Schuster, 1987. A comprehensive biography through Nixon's resignation from the White House.

Anson, Sam. *Exile: The Unquiet Oblivion of Richard M. Nixon.* New York: Simon & Schuster, 1984. Nixon since his resignation.

Brodie, Fawn, *Richard Nixon: The Shaping of His Character.* Cambridge Mass.: Harvard University Press, 1981. A psychological profile.

Eisenhower, Julie Nixon. *Pat Nixon: The Untold Story.* New York: Zebra Books, 1986. Nixon's daughter discusses family life in the White House.

Morris, Roger. *Richard Milhous Nixon.* New York: Henry Holt, 1990. A critical biography of Nixon from his birth through the Checkers speech.

Nadel, Laurie. *The Biography of Richard Nixon.* New York: Macmillan, 1991. A book for young adults.

Parmet, Herbert. *Richard Nixon and His America.* Boston: Little, Brown, 1990. How Nixon's life illustrates modern political practices.

Randolph, Sallie. *Richard M. Nixon, President.* New York: Walker, 1989. A biography for young adults.

Ripley, C. Peter. *Richard Nixon.* New York: Chelsea House, 1987. Nixon as a world leader; for young adults.

Wicker, Tom. *One of Us: Richard Nixon and the American Dream.* New York: Random House, 1991. What Nixon's presidency tells us about American society and politics.

Wills, Garry. *Nixon Agonistes: The Crisis of the Self-Made Man.* Boston: Houghton Mifflin, 1969. An exploration of Nixon's psychology.

NIXON'S MEMOIRS

Nixon, Richard M. *In the Arena: A Memoir of Victory, Defeat, and Renewal.* New York: Simon & Schuster, 1991. Nixon reflects on the meaning of his life in politics.

———. *RN: The Memoirs of Richard Nixon.* 2 vols. New York: Warner Books, 1978. The White House years.

———. *Six Crises.* New York: Doubleday, 1962. Major events prior to Nixon's presidency.

NIXON'S AIDES' MEMOIRS

Erlichman, John D. *Witness to Power.* New York: Pocket Books, 1982. Nixon's political battles and the Watergate crisis.

Haldeman, H. R. *The Ends of Power.* New York: Times Books, 1978. Memoirs of Nixon's chief of staff.

Klein, Herbert G. *Making It Perfectly Clear.* Garden City, N.Y.: Doubleday, 1980. Nixon's director of communications recounts his strategy in dealing with journalists.

Price, Raymond. *With Nixon.* New York: Viking, 1977. The Nixon White House.

Safire, William. *Before the Fall: An Inside View of the Pre-Watergate White House.* New York: Ballantine, 1977. A top speechwriter recalls battles over politics and policies.

PRESIDENTIAL POLICIES

Hersh, Seymour. *The Price of Power: Kissinger in the Nixon White House.* New York: Summit, 1983. A critical profile of Henry Kissinger.

Kissinger, Henry. *White House Years.* Boston: Little, Brown, 1979. An account of Nixon's foreign policy achievements. By his national security advisor.

———. *Years of Upheaval.* Boston: Little, Brown, 1982. An account of how Watergate and domestic crises affected the making of foreign policy in Nixon's second term. By his secretary of state.

Moynihan, Daniel P. *The Politics of a Guaranteed Annual Income: The Nixon Administration and the Family Assistance Plan.* New York: Random House, 1974. The failure of the Nixon proposals for a guaranteed minimum income for the poor.

Newhouse, John. *Cold Dawn: The Story of SALT.* New York: Holt, Rinehart and Winston, 1973. Arms control negotiations in the Nixon years.

Shawcross, William. *Sideshow: Nixon and the Destruction of Cambodia.* New York: Simon & Schuster, 1979. The decision to bomb and invade Cambodia.

WATERGATE

Bernstein, Carl, and Bob Woodward. *All the President's Men.* New York: Simon & Schuster, 1974.

Cohen, Richard M., and Jules Witcover. *A Heartbeat Away.* New York: Viking, 1974. The resignation of Vice President Spiro Agnew during the Watergate crisis.

Drew, Elizabeth. *Washington Journal: The Events of 1973–1974.* New York: Random House, 1976. A Washington reporter's account of the Watergate scandals.

Kutler, Stanley. *The Wars of Watergate: The Last Crisis of Richard Nixon.* New York: Knopf, 1990. A massive, authoritative account.

Lucas, J. Anthony. *Nightmare: The Underside of the Nixon Years.* New York: Viking, 1976. A *New York Times* reporter's account of spying and surveillance during the Nixon presidency.

Sirica, John J. *To Set the Record Straight: The Break-In, the Tapes, the*

Conspirators, the Pardon. New York: Signet, 1980. Memoirs of the judge who tried the Watergate cases.

U.S. House of Representatives Committee on the Judiciary. *Impeachment of Richard M. Nixon, President of the United States. Final Report.* New York: Bantam, 1975.

U.S. Senate Select Committee on Presidential Activities. *Final Report.* New York: Dell, 1974.

White, Theodore H. *Breach of Faith: The Fall of Richard Nixon.* New York: Atheneum/Reader's Digest Press, 1975. Account by a noted Washington reporter.

INDEX

Adams, Duque and Hazeltine, 46
Adams, John, 29
Adams, Sherman, 33
Agnew, Spiro, 53–54, 57, 86–87
Ambrose, Stephen, 65
Arms control, 69
Atkins, Ollie, 93

Blacks, viii, 7, 41, 54, 55, 72–75
Bork, Robert H., 88
Breach of Faith (White), 98
Brezhnev, Leonid, 68, 69, 70
Brown, Edmund "Pat," 46, 47, 52
Burger, Warren E., 91
Bush, George, 37, 97
Busing, 72, 74
Butterfield, Alexander, 85
Byrd, Harry, 45

California, 12, 18–19, 23, 45, 46–47, 56, 58
Cambodia, 62, 64
Campaign funding laws, 85–86
Carter, Jimmy, 99
Central Intelligence Agency (CIA), 83, 90, 91, 95
Chambers, Whittaker, 16–18, 46

Chapin, Dwight, 58
China, 53, 61, 64–68, 69, 70, 97, 98
Chotiner, Murray, 25
CIA *see* Central Intelligence Agency
Civil rights, 14, 21, 40, 41, 55, 71–74
Civil Rights Act of 1964, 71
Cold war, 70
Colson, Charles, 83
Committee of 100, 12
Committee to Re-Elect the President (CREEP), 81, 82–83, 84, 86
Communism, 13, 16, 18–19, 21, 47, 53, 68
Cox, Archibald, 87–89
Crosley, George, 17

Détente, 64, 70
Dean, John W. III, 85, 86
Debates, 42–43
Democratic National Committee, 81, 82, 84
Democratic National Convention (Chicago), 56
Department of Health, Education and Welfare (HEW), 73
Desegregation, 73
Douglas, Helen Gahagan, 18, 52

109

Dulles, John Foster, 33, 36, 47, 66

Eisenhower, Dwight D., 22–25, 30, 33, 34, 36, 37, 39, 40, 43, 46, 47, 52, 53, 57
Ellsberg, Daniel, 86
Enemies list, 82, 86, 98
Equal Pay Act of 1963, 75
Erlichman, John D., 83, 85, 89
Ervin, Sam, 85
Executive privilege, 85

FBI *see* Federal Bureau of Investigation
Federal Bureau of Investigation (FBI), 82, 84, 88, 90, 95
Ford, Gerald R., 87, 93, 96, 97, 99
Foreign affairs, 14, 51, 71, 93
Fourteen Point Compact of Fifth Avenue, 39
Frost, David, 96

Gender discrimination, 75–76
Goldwater, Barry, 39, 50, 53, 91
Great Depression, 7, 8
Great Wall of China, 66, 67
Gromyko, Andrei, 69

Hagerty, Jim, 33
Haldeman, H. R., 82, 83, 85, 89
Hall, Len, 45
Hanoi (Vietnam), 62, 63
Hearst, William Randolph, Jr., 91
Hegemony, 68
Hiss, Alger, 16–18
House Committee on Un-American Activities (HUAC), 16–17
House Judiciary Committee, 91, 95
Humphrey, Hubert, 37, 56, 57, 58–59

Hungary, 29
Hunger, 78
Hunt, E. Howard, Jr., 81, 83

Illinois, 45, 56, 58
Internal Revenue Service (IRS), 86, 90, 95

Jaworski, Leon, 91
Jobs, 74–75
John Birch Society, 47
Johnson, Lyndon Baines, 41, 50, 51, 55–56, 57–58, 62, 73, 79
Justice Department, 84, 85

Kennedy, John F., 37, 40, 41–45, 50, 52, 62, 71
Kennedy, Robert F., 56
Krushchev, Nikita, 31, 32, 38
King, Martin Luther, Jr., 55
Kissinger, Henry, 63, 64–65, 65, 68–70
"Kitchen debate," 32
Kleindienst, Richard, 85
Knowland, William, 22
Korea, 28, 58
Kosygin, Alexei, 68

Latin America, 30
Liddy, G. Gordon, 82–83
Lima (Peru), 30
Local government, 78–79
Lodge, Henry Cabot, 40

The Making of the President: 1960 (White), 39
Malnutrition, 78
Mao Zedong, 65, 66

INDEX

Marcantonio, Vito, 18–19
Marshall, George C., 14
Marshall Plan, 14
Matz, Lester, 86
McCarthy, Eugene, 55, 56
McCord, James W., Jr., 82
McGovern, George, 84
Media, 52
Michigan, 44–45, 56, 58
Milhous family, 1–2
Milhous, Hannah *see* Nixon, Hannah
Minority-owned businesses, 75
Mitchell, John, 73, 83, 84, 85
Mitchell, Stephen, 24
Mondale, Walter, 37
Morris, Roger, 10
Moynihan, Daniel Patrick, 76
Mudge, Rose, Guthrie and Alexander, 49

National Security Council, 33
New Federalism, 79
New Hampshire, 52, 55
New York, 56, 58
New York Bar Association, 95
Nixon, Arthur, 5
Nixon, Donald, 3, 4
Nixon, Frank, 2, 3, 4, 7
Nixon, Hannah, 1–2, 4, 5, 7
Nixon, Harold, 4, 5, 7
Nixon, Julie, 13, 26, 46, 93
Nixon, Pat, 9–10, 12, 26, 27, 46, 47, 51, 65, 67, 96, 97
Nixon, Richard
  Checkers speech, 23–27
  and China, 64–68, 97, 98
  college and law school, 7–8
  comeback trail, 95–99

  as congressman, 14–18
  disgrace, 91–93
  domestic policy, 71–79
  early years, 3–7
  family tree, 1–3
  finances, 96
  first campaign, 12–14
  first presidential campaign, 37–45
  gubernatorial race, 46–47
  impeachment proceedings, 89–90
  inauguration, vii, 61
  interest in politics, 5, 7, 8
  Kennedy debates, 42–43
  as lawyer, 8–9, 49
  Library and Birthplace, 97
  marriage, 10
  Moscow summit, 68–70
  pardon, 96
  reelection to presidency, 84
  resignation, viii, 93
  schooling, 3, 5
  second presidential campaign, 51–54, 56–59
  Senate campaign, 18–19
  as senator, 21
  service in Pacific, 11–12
  tapes, 87–89, 91
  travels, 29–32, 65–67
  as vice-president, 29–37
  vice-presidential campaign, 21–27
  and Vietnam War, 57–58, 61–64, 97
  Watergate affair, 81–86, 89, 91, 96
Nixon, Tricia, 13, 26
Nixon family, 2
Nuclear weapons, 69

O'Brien, Lawrence, 82

Office of Economic Opportunity (OEO), 77
Office of Price Administration (OPA), 10, 11
Ohio, 56, 58
Operation Gemstone, 82, 84
Operation Mercy, 29
Oregon, 53

Paris Peace Accords, 64
Pennsylvania, 57, 58
Percy, Charles, 52
Perry, Herman, 12
Philadelphia (Pa.), 74
Philadelphia Plan, 75
Poverty, 77–78
Powers, Francis Gary, 38

Quakers, 1, 2, 7, 11

Reagan, Ronald, 52, 53, 56, 96, 97
Religion, 41
Republic Committee on Program and Progress, 39
Republication National Committee, 25, 27, 51
Republican Party, 12, 13, 14, 34, 39, 50, 51
Reston, James, 63
Richard Milhous Nixon: The Rise of an American Politician (Morris), 10
Richardson, Elliot L., 87, 88
Rockefeller, Nelson, 38–40, 50, 52, 53, 56
Rogers, William, 33
Romney, George, 52
Roosevelt, Franklin D., 9, 13, 14
Ruckelshaus, William D., 88

Ryan, Pat *see* Nixon, Pat

Saturday Night Massacre, 89
Saxbe, William, 63
Scott, Hugh, 91
Select Committee on Nutrition and Human Needs, 78
Shanghai communiqué, 66
Shultz, George, 73, 74
Sirhan, Sirhan, 56
Sirica, John, 84, 87
Six Crises (Nixon), 23, 25, 26, 30, 33, 34, 36, 38, 39, 46, 66
Smith, Dana, 23–24
Southern states, 41, 58
Soviet Union, 29–32, 38, 53, 61, 64, 68–70, 97, 98
Sparkman, John, 27
State Department, 16, 17
State government, 78–79
State and Local Fiscal Assistance Act, 79
Stevenson, Adlai, 27
Supreme Court, 90–91

Taft, Robert, 22, 23
Taft–Hartley Labor Act, 14
Taiwan, 65
Texas, 45, 57, 58
Thieu, Nguyen van, 62
Thurmond, Strom, 53
Truman, Harry S, 14

United Nations, 16, 65
United States v. *Nixon*, 90

Venezuela, 30
Vietnam War, vii, 51, 55, 56, 57–58,

INDEX

61–64, 65, 68, 84, 97
Voorhis, Jerry, 12, 13
Voting Rights Act of 1965, 71–72

Wallace, George, 56, 58–59
Warren, Earl, vii, 22, 23, 24
Watergate affair, 81–86, 89, 91, 96
Welfare reform, 76–77
White, Theodore, 39, 40, 43, 98
Whittier (Calif.), 2, 9
Whittier College, 7
Whittier Young Republicans, 9
Wilkins, Roy, 73
Wills, Frank, 81
Wingert and Bewley, 8
Wiretapping, 82, 85, 87, 98
Women, 75–76
Woods, Rosemary, 51
World War II, 10–12
Writings of Mao Zedong, 66

Years of Upheaval (Kissinger), 64

Zhou En-lai, 64, 65, 66
Ziegler, Ronald L., 82

PHOTO ACKNOWLEDGMENTS

AP/Wide World: 42, 67. National Archives: 4, 6, 15, 26, 31, 35, 54, 72, 83, 92. *Washington Star*: 88.

About the Author

Richard M. Pious is a professor of political science at Barnard College and the Graduate Faculties of Columbia University, where he has taught since 1968. He is the author of *The American Presidency; The President, Congress and the Constitution*; and the textbook *American Politics and Government*. He is also the author of the article on President Nixon in *The Encyclopedia of the American Presidency*. Professor Pious was the editor of the Academy of Political Science's centennial volume, *The Power to Govern*, and is the editor of the Dabor reprint series of classic works in American constitutional law and a fifteen-volume reprint series of classic journal articles on the presidency. His articles have appeared in *Political Science Quarterly, Journal of International Affairs, Wisconsin Law Review*, and the *Journal of Armed Forces and Society*. He is also a frequent contributor to *Current History*. Professor Pious has participated in numerous seminars for high school history and social studies teachers run by the Taft Institute and the New-York Historical Society and funded by the National Endowment for the Humanities.